Today´s
COUNTRY HOUSES

Edition 2005

Author: Jacobo Krauel
Publisher: Carles Broto
Editorial Coordinator: Jacobo Krauel
Architectural Advisor: Pilar Chueca
Graphic designer & production: Dimitris Kottas
Text: contributed by the architects, edited by Núria Rodríguez and
William George

© Carles Broto i Comerma
Jonqueres, 10, 1-5
08003 Barcelona, Spain
Tel.: +34 93 301 21 99
 Fax: +34-93-301 00 21
E-mail: info@linksbooks.net
www. linksbooks.net

Today´s
COUNTRY HOUSES

INDEX

INTRODUCTION

The city is a centre of wealth, culture and trade. It is also the place where dwellings and workplaces are usually concentrated, and therefore, it is the most common context for the development of architecture. More and more people, however, have decided to move to the country in search of the contact with nature and the tranquillity of a life far from the bustle of the city. As a reaction to the urban masses, there is a growing tendency to return to the traditional life by rehabilitating isolated buildings in rural areas, paying greater attention to the environment surrounding the dwelling and seeking privileged views that can be enjoyed from any part of the house. This residential unit par excellence is the architectural form that most lends itself to creative activity -it is the framework in which privacy is built and invented. Despite the invasion of the media and the existence of stereotyped behaviours and fashions, the home is still the only place that is designed and decorated in privacy, the place that reflects the individual's fight against normalisation and standardisation, and the need to express a difference, an identity. The house is a place of rest -and nowadays even a place of work, as home offices and workshops replace those that characterised the industrial revolution.

This volume offers a representative selection of the forms of construction of country houses by some of the most prestigious contemporary architects. They all show a respect for nature -some even introduce ecological innovations in the construction- and pay great attention to the treatment of light and view. There is also a common desire to integrate the dwellings into the landscape through the use of materials and colours. Though they persistently seek a relationship with the landscape, all the works presented here show different solutions that respond to the different needs of their inhabitants, to their culture, values and beliefs, and to the physical and climatic context of the location. Through constant attention to the client brief, the composition and the construction, these proposals revive the dialogue between the dwelling and the surrounding nature.

Mack Scogin Merril Elam Architects
Mountain Tree House

Dillard, Georgia, USA

This project is an addition of a guesthouse, a bamboo deck and a garage to an older house. The house is a weekend retreat into the vertical poplar trunks among the Appalachian Mountains.

The garage is used for working, gardening, for the storage of tools and the occasional car. It is walled by unfinished concrete, with plain doors and long windows. The bedroom above is cantilevered over the work-yard. In contrast to the closed volume of the garage, the bedroom is open with glass walls. The little bathroom is solid and clad in steel. The walls swing open for outdoor showers and spring cleaning. The bamboo is planted in planters on the ground and grows through narrow slots in the deck above. This space is for sitting and viewing in and among the fast growing canes.

The structure of the deck and the guesthouse is made of wood and steel. The surface of the deck and the interior floor are black slate. The ramp and the handrails are made of self-weathered steel. Panels of the same steel are used in the cladding of the upper room. The glass walls consist of either clear tempered or translucent laminated glass.

Photographs: Timothy Hursley, The Arkansas Office

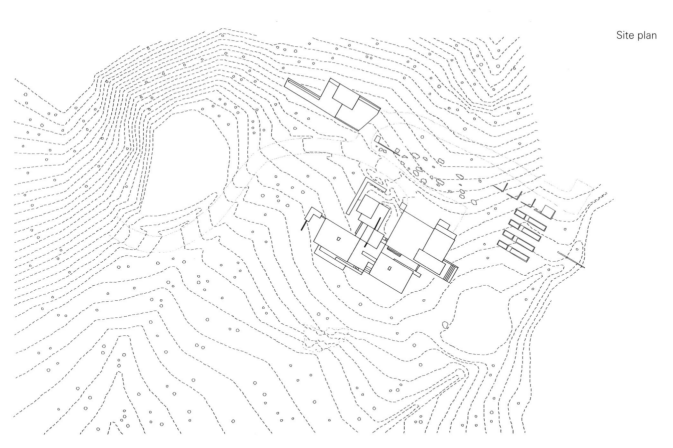

Site plan

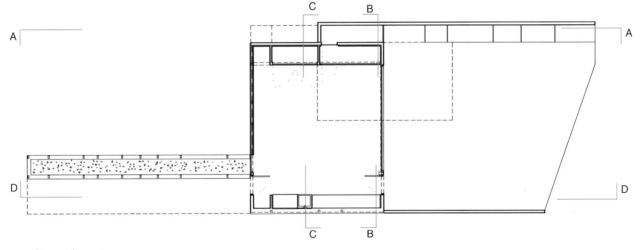

Ground floor plan

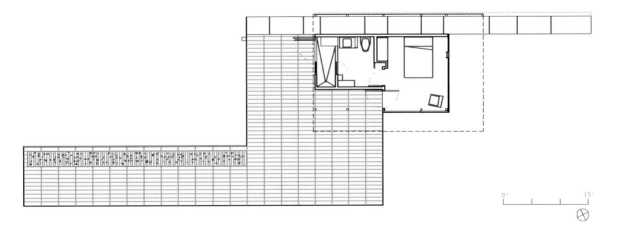

First floor plan

Section AA

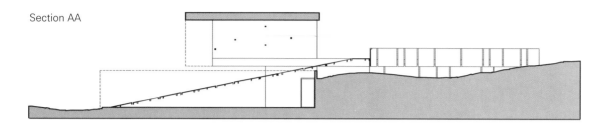

Section BB

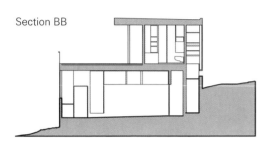

Section CC

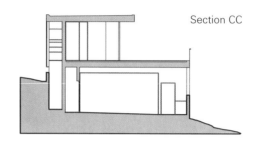

Section DD

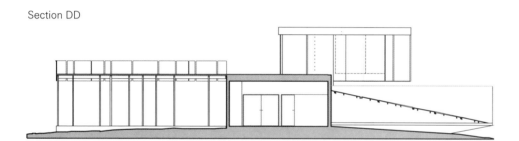

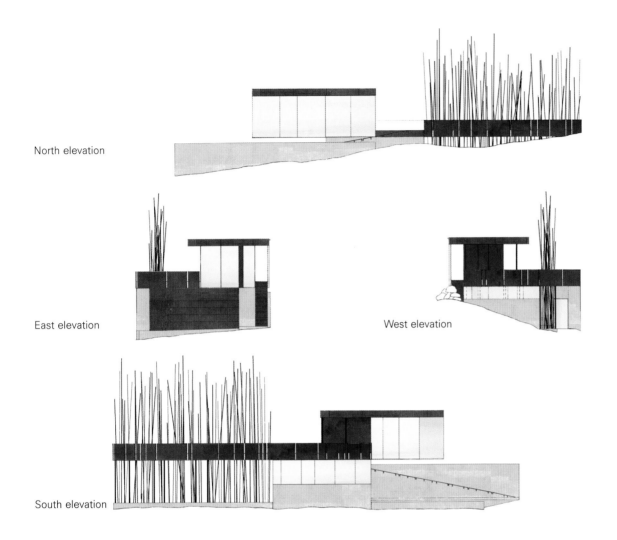

North elevation

East elevation

West elevation

South elevation

The structure of the guesthouse is wood and steel. The interior floor is black slate. Steel panels are used in the cladding of the room. The glass walls consist of either clear tempered or translucent laminated glass.

Felipe Assadi Figueroa
Schmitz House

Calera de Tango, Chile

This project is a country house at Calera de Tango on a 4.5 ha site, for a couple with no children. The land is planted with small fruit trees and has a view of the cordillera de Los Andes to the east and the coast to the west. The south and north are determined by closer sights of eucalyptus.

The sight and the rhythm of the fruit trees propose a direction and size for the project. Their foliage, at one meter high, creates a new ground level.

These characteristics of the land together with the idea of artificial occupation that creates a dialogue of contrasts creates the basic scheme of two volumes and a foundation wall. This one - a concrete box 1 meter high and 2.7 meters wide upon the east-west center point, contains the swimming pool and the basement and constitutes the foundations of the house at the same time.

Over this base, at the height of the trees, the first volume contains the public program, inside a rectangular volume made out of glass and larch. Using the north-south axis, the second volume, made from untreated concrete, hangs out of the glass box producing a new contrast effect, this time vertically.

Through the sunlight, the green glass creates colors, transparency and reflections, creating, in the exterior, a changing dialogue with the landscape. From the inside, the spatial limits extend to the trees so that the interior space is determined by the surrounding landscape.

The axis of the foundation, constituted by the swimming pool, the basement and the stairs, connects the two volumes to the earth through a perforated wall that creates a communication between the spaces that it divides.

The materials that have been used are: exposed concrete, larch wood, green glass and steel.

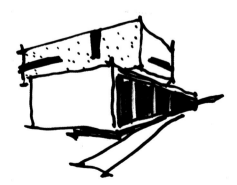 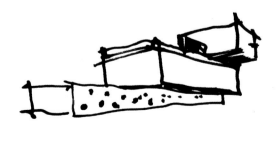

Photographs: contributed by the architect

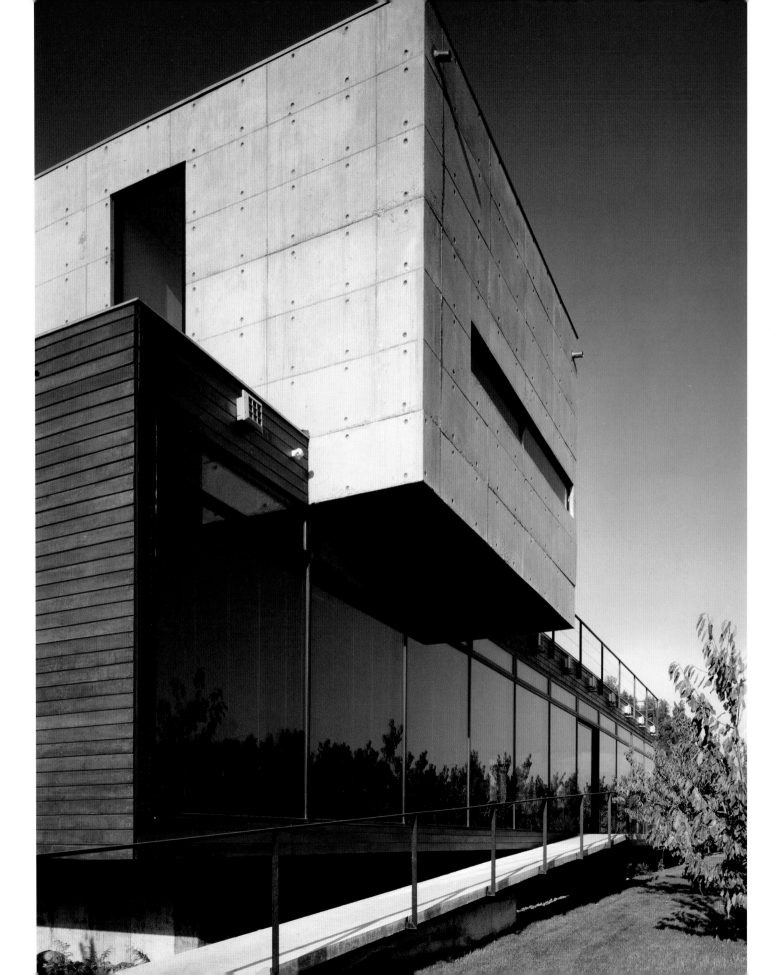

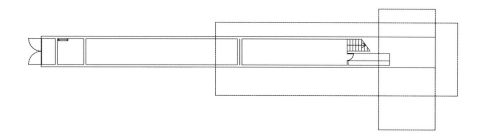

Ground floor plan

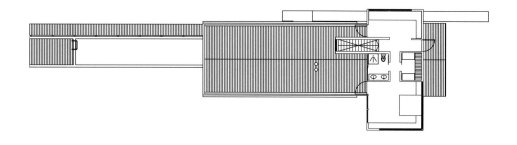

First floor plan

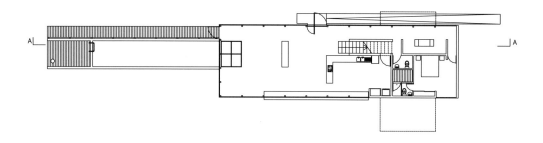

Second floor plan

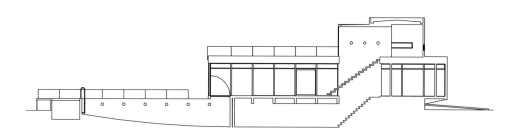

Section AA

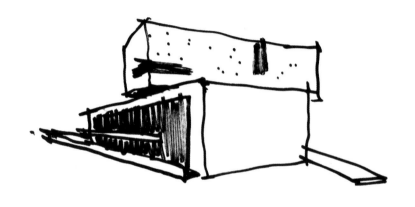

The openings on the volumes are placed according to the desired degree of privacy for each space. The living room is totally transparent while the main bedroom is mostly opaque.

HERTL.ARCHITEKTEN
Steinwendtner House

Steyr-Münichholz, Austria

The Steinwendtner House in Steyr-Münchholz was planned as a low-cost single-family house. The whole building is a timber construction, only the two containers in the garden that are used as a garage for bikes and also for garden tools are made of steel. In order to compensate for the smaller floor space the architect doubled the use of the aisle region as a passageway-room that is connected to the different rooms.

Once inside the house, one still can feel the volume of the whole building, a spaciousness that cannot be understood from the outside. The owners wanted a house protected from the views from the street. The solid façade of the south wall protects from view while the large glass wall of the first floor brings the southern daylight down in the living area. On the north side, the living area opens into the green of the nearby forest through a terrace that was cut out of the body of the building.

The analogy of the light-atmosphere to sacred places is throughout wanted.

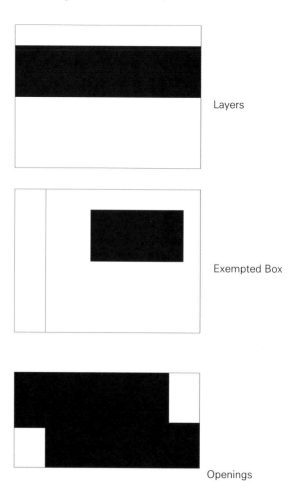

Layers

Exempted Box

Openings

Photographs: Paul Ott

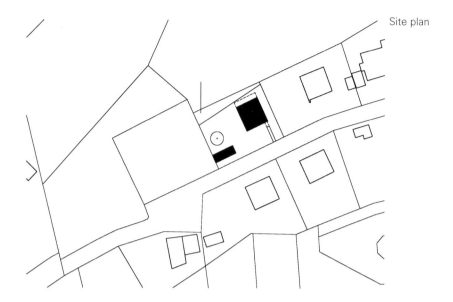
Site plan

The Steinwendtner House in Steyr-Münchholz is a low-cost single-family house. The whole building is a timber construction.

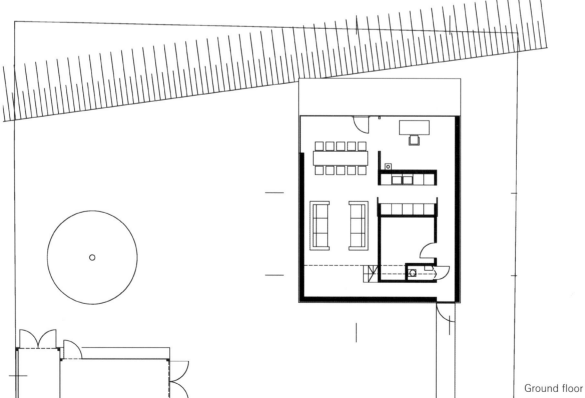

Ground floor

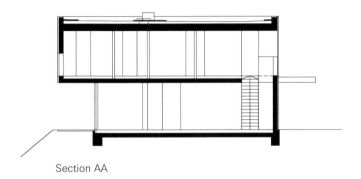

Section AA

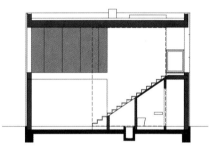

Section 11

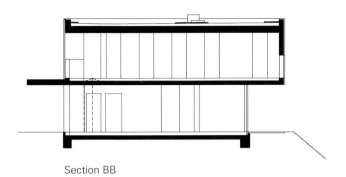

Section BB

Section 22

First floor

Southeast elevation

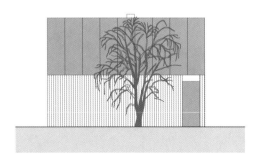

Northeast elevation

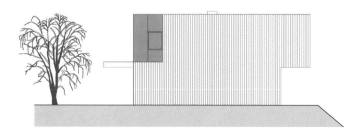

Northwest elevation   Southwest elevation

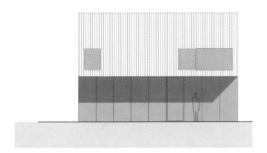

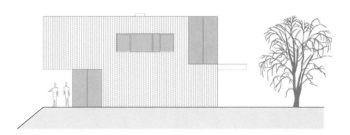

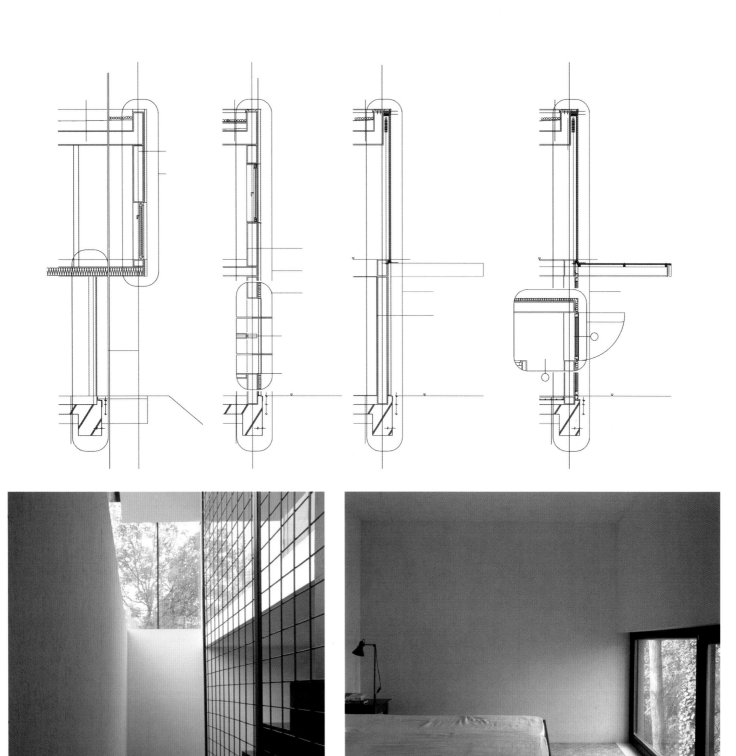

The living area receives southern light from the large glass wall of the first floor. On the ground floor, the south façade is closed to protect the living room from street views.

Luis Ibarra and Teresa Rosano
Gracia House

Tucson, Arizona, USA

The site of the Gracia house is a steep north-facing slope in the foothills of the Tucson Mountains with commanding views of city lights and the surrounding mountains. The architects decided to design a structure that would appear to grow out of the rocky desert landscape without dominating it. They spent a long time on the site studying the sightlines, topography, plants, animal paths, winds and solar angles.

The axis of the house is set parallel with the site contours. Three narrow bays have been created to terrace up the hill, keeping the excavation and fill to a minimum. The terracing platforms contain the three zones of the house: living, circulating and sleeping.

The circulation bay in the middle contains the entrance and functions also as an extension of the living spaces. It is axially aligned with mountain peaks so that the openings at each end frame the views. This space invites visitors down to the living area of the lowest platform while connecting it with the upper platform that contains the bedrooms.

The main axis of the house is rotated on the living room so that the main window faces the fantastic views of the Tucson city lights and the Catalina Mountains.

The south sun is introduced to the living spaces by splitting the bedrooms apart and creating a small intimate courtyard.

West facing glass surfaces have been kept to the minimum. Horizontal and vertical openings punctuate the block volumes throughout, highlighting the views. Corner windows frame the city lights in the master bedroom and the mountain ridge in the laundry room.

The material palette consists of simple durable materials that respond to the desert climate, colors and textures. The walls are Integra® Block, an insulated concrete block system. The sandblasted surface of the blocks is the finishing material for both interior and exterior so that their distinction is blurred. Rusted steel echoes the iron oxide coloring found in the fieldstone while steel plate steps zigzag between the different concrete floor levels and birch plywood cabinets provide function and warmth.

Photographs: Bill Timmerman

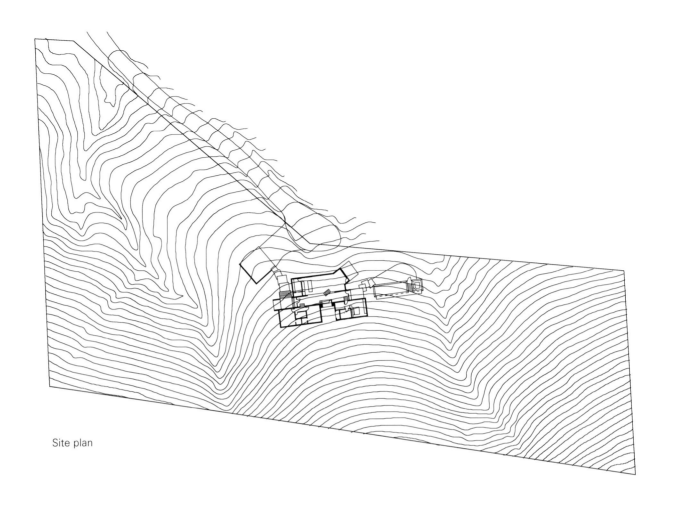

Site plan

45

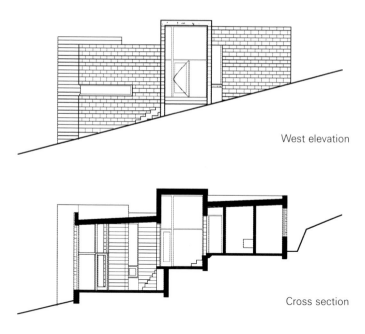

West elevation

Cross section

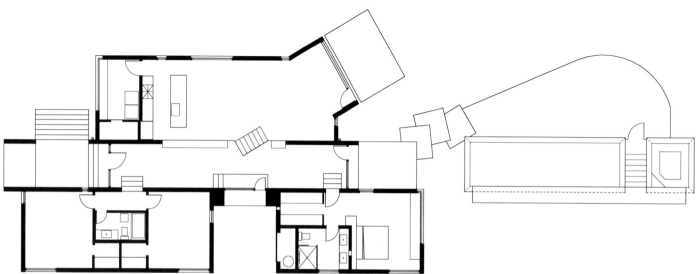

In order to bring the southern sunlight into the rooms, the bedrooms have been split and a small courtyard has been created in the middle. This courtyard serves as a sheltered exterior room with a secret garden with brightly painted fuchsia walls and colorful bougainvillea.

The main axis of the living room has been turned so that the main window (opposite page) faces the views of the city and the mountains. Here the edge of the dwelling meets the desert floor, giving inhabitants a feeling of shelter and a connection to the land. Regularly, a resident pack of javelina (a wild-pig like animal) comes into the foreground to peer through the window at the owners.

Engelen Moore

The Rose House

This house is located south of Sydney on a rural lot on the southern side of Saddleback Mountain, approximately 50m below the summit. The site is convex in form with a ridge running north-south down the center, falling 15 meters towards the bush line.

The rectangular plan form is divided into three zones by way of two service cores. The eastern zone is for the parents, the western zone for the children, while in the center is the kitchen, living and dining area. By centralizing the living areas and pulling the service cores back from the glazing lines there are significant diagonal vistas in all directions. As there is also a significant view to the East a horizontal window has been introduced in the main bedroom wall above the bed. This window is shaded with adjustable external aluminum louvers. There is an open platform with an aluminum louvered roof to the north of the living areas which forms the entry to the house as well as a shaded verandah. On entering the house the dramatic view down the mountain to the south is instantly apparent.

The use of two Vierendeel trusses running the length of the house allows the house to cantilever 3.5 meters beyond the storerooms at the east and west ends, with the 460 UB bottom chord fully expressed at the underside of the concrete floor slab. The 2 service cores pass through the floor down to ground level, providing the bracing to the structure. These cores also conceal all plumbing and provide storage areas beneath the house. The roof and end walls are clad in the same grey profiled steel sheeting. The window and door system consists of identical sliding aluminum framed glass doors on both the north and south elevations, with adjustable glass louvers above on the north elevation.

Photographs: Ross Honeysett

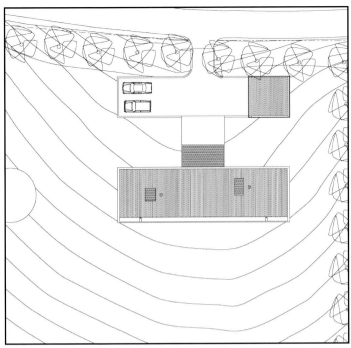

Site plan

In order to maximize the views and build on the site's gentler slope, the house has been set adjacent to the road at the upper edge of the plot and centered on the north-south ridge to take advantage of an almost symmetrical fall to both the east and west..

North elevation

South elevation

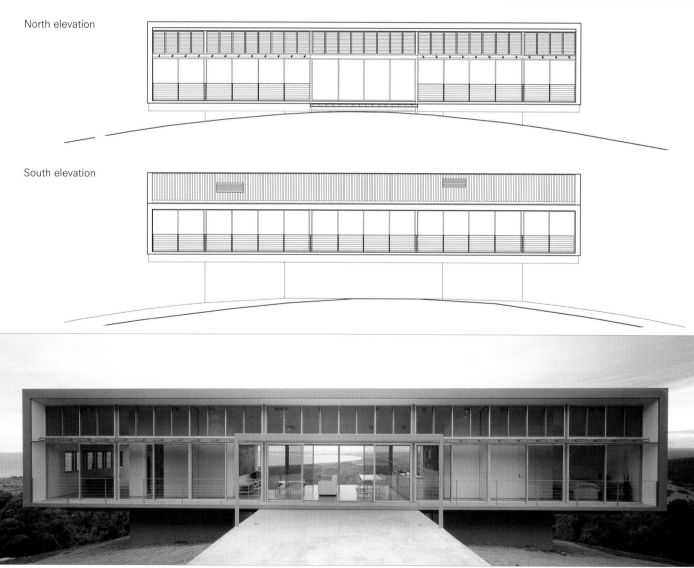

East elevation

West elevation

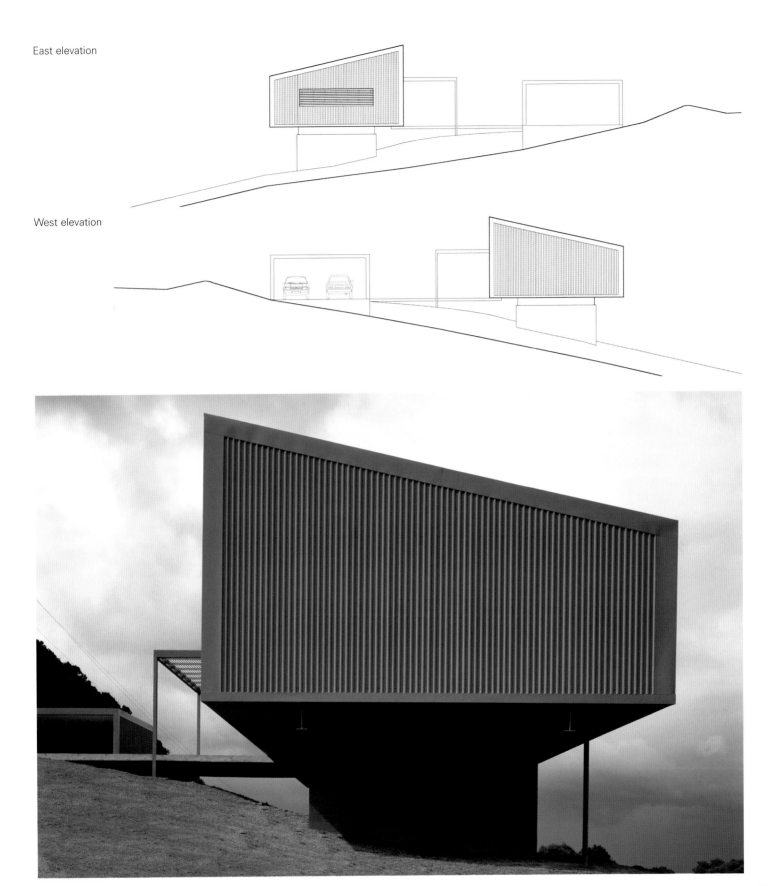

Cross section

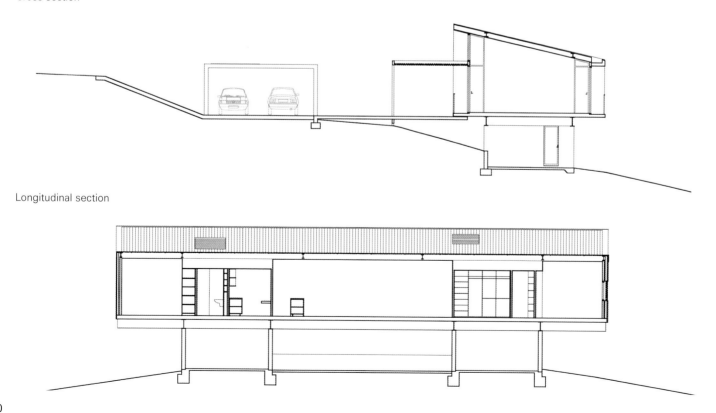

Longitudinal section

There are 800-millimeter-wide decks running the length of the house on the north and the south, thereby providing sun shading and weather protection for the large sliding glass walls. When the doors are open the entire living area becomes an open verandah space with exceptional cross ventilation.

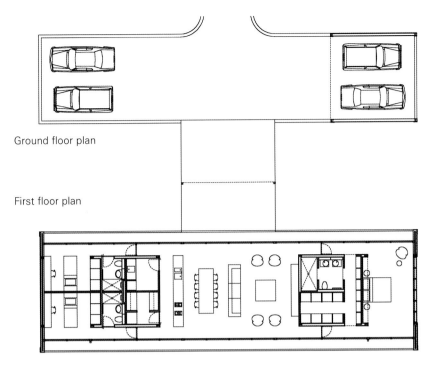

Ground floor plan

First floor plan

In order to minimize the impact of the building, the architect has employed a lightweight steel structure consisting of 2 Vierendeel trusses running the length of the house and sitting on 2 reinforced concrete block storerooms, which form the only contact with the ground. The trusses allow the house to cantilever 3.5 meters beyond the storerooms at the east and west ends.

Florian Nagler Architekten
House and Studio Lang-Kröll

Gleissenberg, Germany

Near Cham, between the Bavarian Forest and the Böhmerwald, the clients wanted a house for themselves and their four children. The artist Peter Lang, who works mainly with large-sized woodcuts, required a studio to contain both a painting area and his printing machines. The project was molded by the low budget, and by the great architectural open-mindedness of the clients and of the local authorities.

In a rather trivial development-area on the outskirts of Gleissenberg, the building's geometry fits in with the buildings nearby. The wood-frame construction rests upon a basement-plinth, formed by two walls of fairfaced concrete that run parallel to the contour lines. It was assembled using 14 prefabricated floor and wall units of different sizes, the largest being 4.10 m x 12.48 m. The cantilever rests on beams that are part of the ground floor's inner walls. The floor units bear on these walls and are bolted together. Some shortwalls above the concrete walls in the basement take over the crossbracing.

The entrance, heating installation and workshop are located in the basement. The cantilever shelters an exterior space around the front door, that is used as a carport and storage area for the firewood used as heating fuel. The ground floor contains all the domestic space, and the studio is above it, under the self-supporting gabled roof. The home has a neutral floor plan, so the young family can adapt their living area as required.

The façade is a double wall of transparent polycarbonate, giving a bright atmosphere to the living quarters and flooding the studio with light. The insulating airspace between the inner and the outer wall-cladding can be switched from summer to winter mode by simply covering the ventilation holes. The ceiling is of rough fir wood, and all the cladding is polycarbonate, and no timber is left exposed to the weather. The simple connector system of the polycarbonate elements and the wood shingle roof enabled the clients to contribute an important share of the labor involved. The building's interior and exterior are the direct results of the constructive systems used, the undisguised materials, and simple, suitable details.

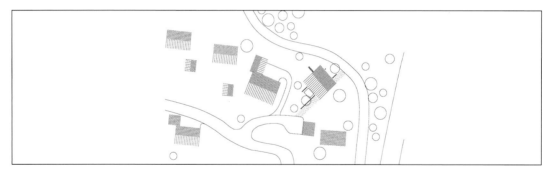

Photographs: Simone Rosenberg

Basement plan

The entrance, heating installation and a workshop are located in the basement. The bulge forms a space, that is used as a roofed access, a carport and storage area for firewood. The ground floor contains all the living areas and the first floor contains the artist´s studio. The house has a neutral floor plan, so the young family is able to enhance their living area, if required.

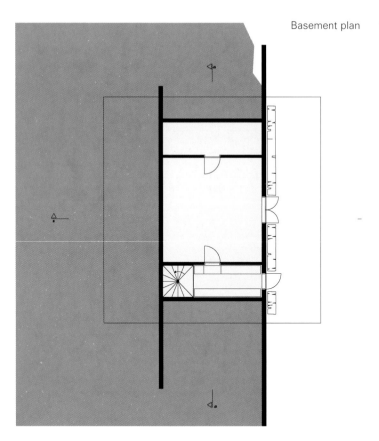

Ground floor plan

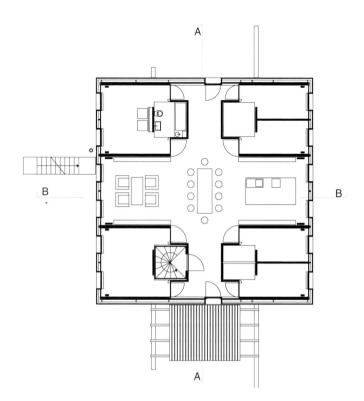

First floor plan

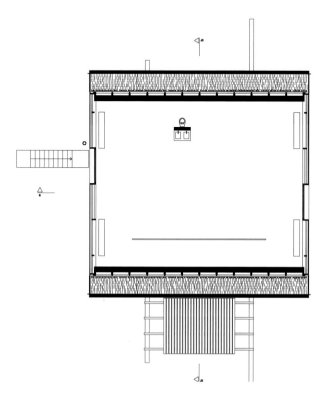

Section AA

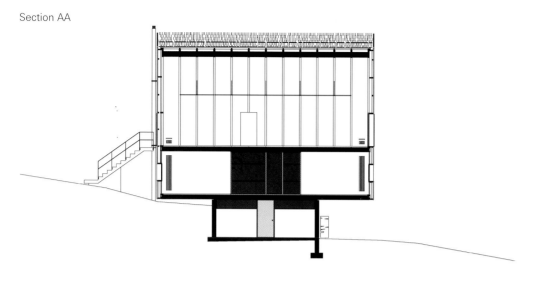

Section BB

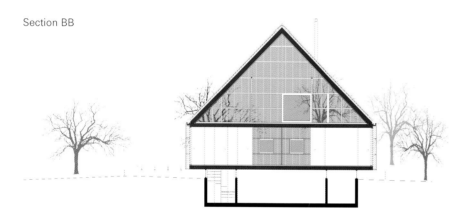

Elevation

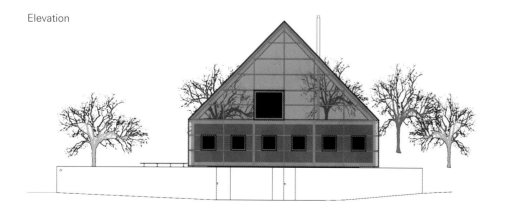

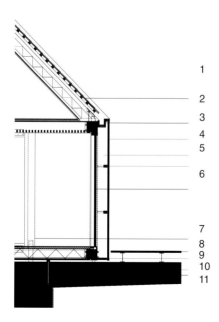

1

2

3

4

5

6

7

8

9

10

11

Section of double wall and roof

1. Clapboard roof
2. Internal gutter
3. Cladding (polycarbonate dual-wall) with breather hotels
4. Clearance
5. Substructure with spacers
6. Wall panels, Gluelam covered with OSB
7. Bracing wall
8. Terrace
9. Deal with ventilation holes
10. Steel anchoring
11. Fanlight

The transparent double wall façade, made of polycarbonate, creates a bright atmosphere in the living area and floods the studio with light. The interspace between the inner and outer façades can be turned from summer to winter function by simply covering the ventilation holes. The ceiling is made of rough fir wood, and all the cladding is polycarbonate, so no timber is left exposed to the weather.

Tham Videgard Hansson Architects
Karlsson House

Tidö-Lindö, Västerås, Sweden

This one family house is situated on the northern coast of the lake Mälaren in central Sweden. It is set in a former recreational area where, in recent years, most of the small weekend houses have been either extended or replaced by catalogue housing.

A starting point has been the simple constructions of rural buildings and the architecture of Swedish barns and warehouses, some traces of which can still be seen within the extensive type house sprawl of Tidö-Lindö. The clients, a couple in their sixties, wanted a house for themselves including space to accommodate visiting children and friends. They had never met an architect before.

The brief was defined in two parts: a complete living floor at entrance level, and an upper floor that is only partly finished representing a future possible extension within the house. Aiming to meet a need for cheap construction the plan is strictly based on a cc1200 module. Due to this and to the use of standard building components the costs were kept extremely low, thirty to fifty percent less than average.

In contrast to the deep red exterior, the interior space is very light. It is characterized by the three light shafts that rise through the attic to let the sunlight enter from above. Two are situated at the short walls of the open living room and the third marks the position of the stair at the south gable. Combining rooms in a suite with transverse passages the plan offers several alternative movements through the house. Windows are placed to further enhance the difference of the interior spaces by alternatingly directing the views low towards the garden, far away towards the lake and the horizon, or high up at the trees and the sky above.

Freely placed windows in two sizes punctuate the roof and the facades. Fixed screen-like shutters complement the varied interior light as well as the pattern of shadow and light of the outside. All exterior fittings and details are painted in the same color as the facade.

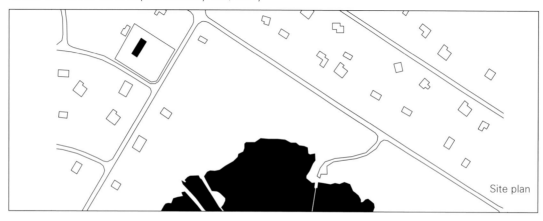

Site plan

Photographs: Åke E:son Lindman

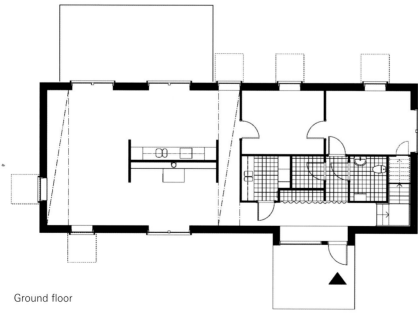

Ground floor

The ground floor contains a complete house. The upper floor is only partly finished and it can function as a space for a possible inner extension of the house.

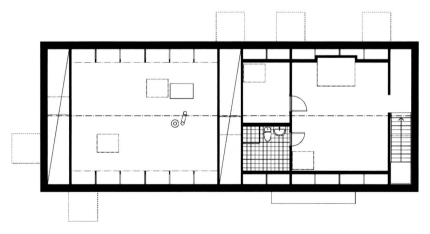

First floor

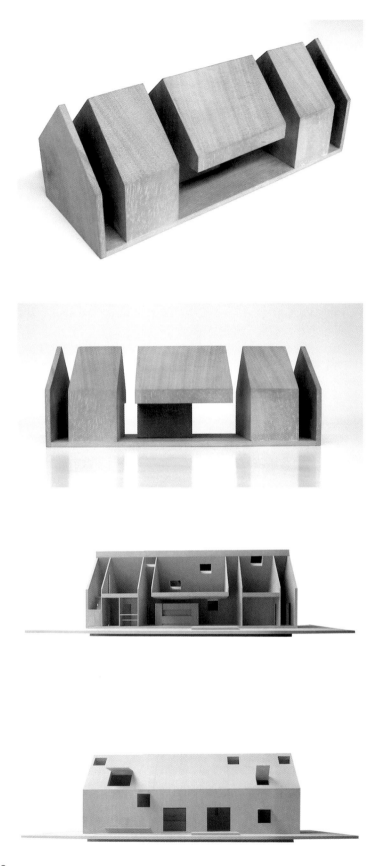

The prismatic exterior is clad with an oversized wooden panel made of heartwood of slowly grown pine and treated with red tar, a way of reinterpreting the technique of wooden roofs that has been in use for centuries in Scandinavia, mostly in the north and on the island of Gotland in the Baltic Sea.

The interior spaces are painted in light colors in contrast to the deep-red exterior. The light comes in from the many different windows that direct the views in different parts of the landscape, like the garden, the lake and the horizon far away, or high up at the trees and the sky above.

Eduardo Souto de Moura
House in Cascais

Cascais, Portugal

This house in Cascais was designed at the same time as another in Azeitão, two houses in the South resolved according to the characteristics of each project. To the architect, the problem faced when designing a house has to do with perceiving the identity of the client and the site, in order to invent a "heteronym". The potential for repetition depends on the context in terms of the possibilities of the moment and the personality of the "place".

In Cascais the context for the house was an immense horizontal ocean, the Atlantic. Because it is impossible to "capture" an ocean, which is always changing yet always the same, the house responds with a neutral gaze. It develops a language of openings, gaps, negative and positive spaces.

The material and the colors are "all different, all the same - grayish". Moving through the house from the exterior to the interior, the shades of gray slowly change, transforming into the whiteness of the cellar.

The gray tones of Azulino Cascais stone, the matt glow of aluminum and sand-polished stainless-steel are waiting for the western wind to transform their "grayish" state.

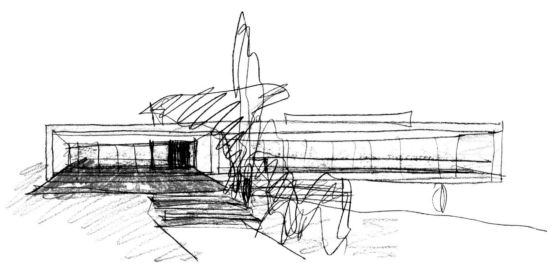

Photographs: Duccio Malagamba

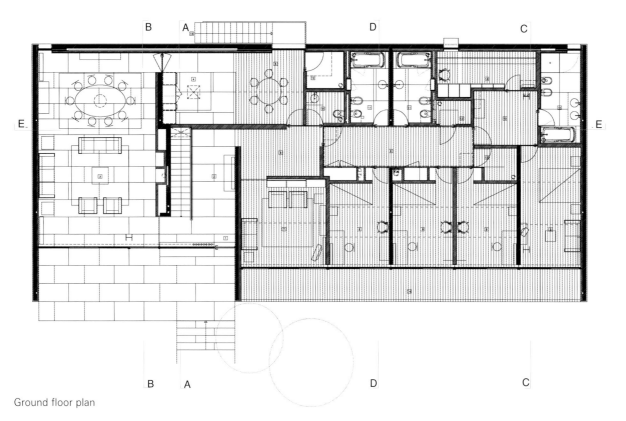

Ground floor plan

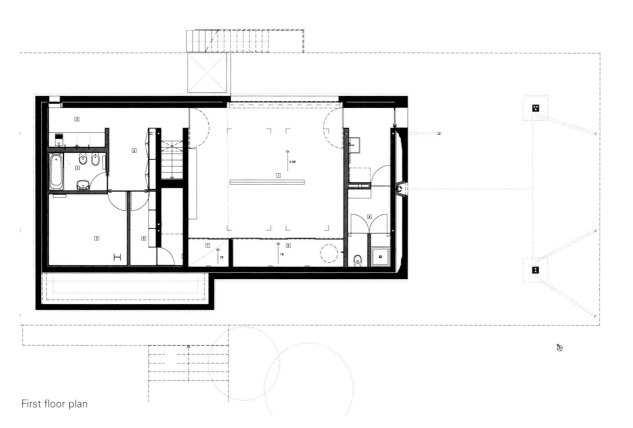

First floor plan

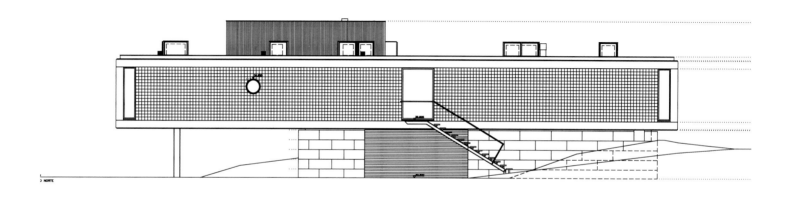

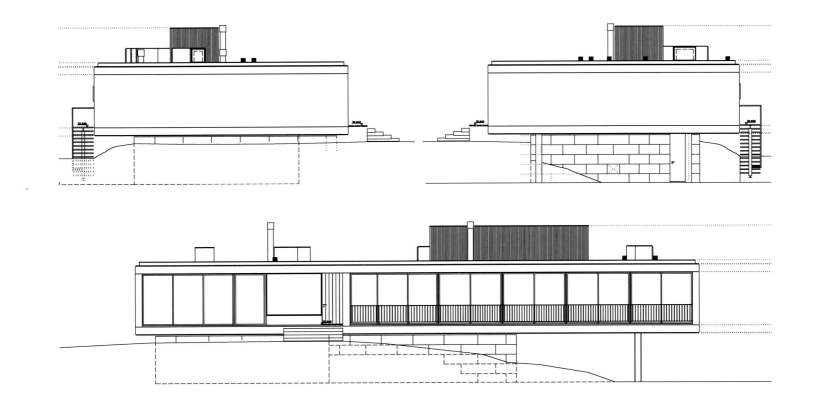

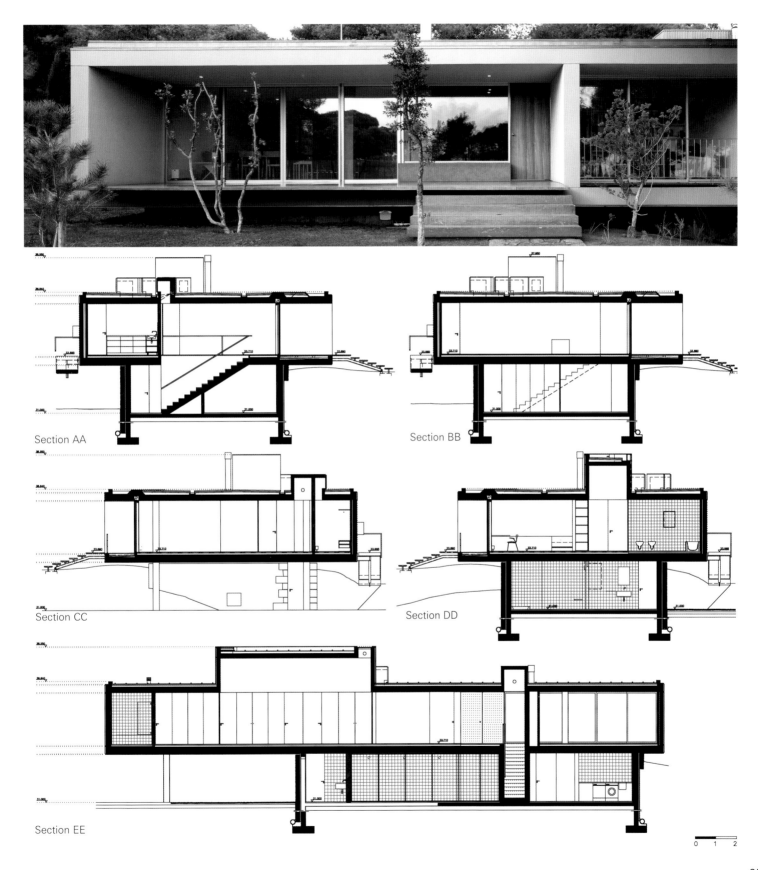

Section AA

Section BB

Section CC

Section DD

Section EE

0 1 2

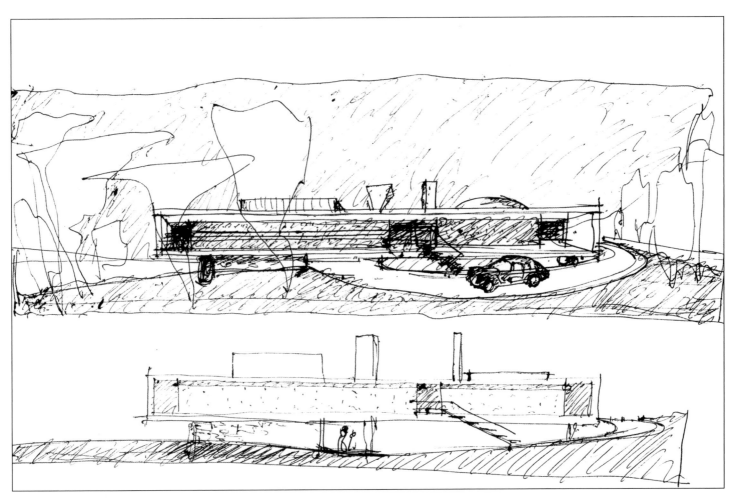

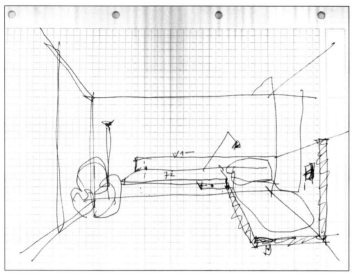

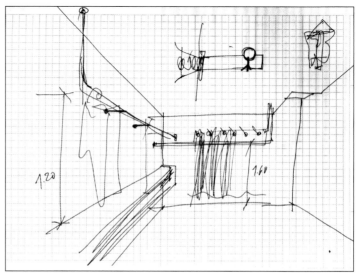

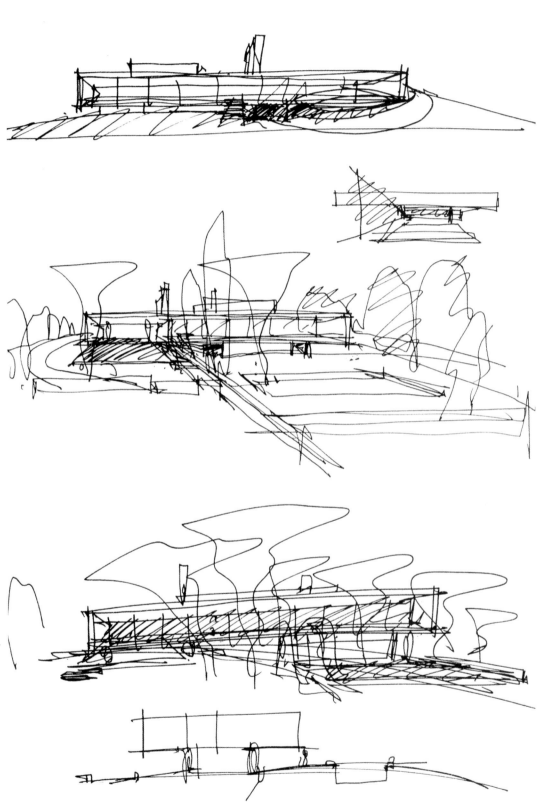

Archi-tectonics
Gypsy Trail Residence

Kent, NY, USA

At Croton Reservoir in upstate New York, The Gypsy Trail residence is built into a lakefront landscape that alternates the soft and hard of leaf, rock and water. The ground floor is built of rough stone collected on site and is partially recessed into the hillside. Perched above the stone base is the cantilevered second floor. This box of steel, wood, and glass sits at an angle to procure a direct view of the lake and capture maximum sunlight, which enters through glass planes integrated into the continuous wall-to-roof surface.

The house's "generative core" originates in the ground floor, achieving its full form and function in the floor above. This core is a centrally located "smart structure" integrating kitchen, bathrooms, fireplace, heating and cooling systems, and music. Morphing of the armature's programmatic elements produces a segmented, organic shape. The armature functions as an infra-structural unit, but also as a circulatory and generative element, directing interior movement and molding the surfaces connected to it, creating the geometry of the house; the roof warps to conform to its segmentation. As the hard exterior surface responds to the generative force of the armature, the box softens, tilts, and fragments. Architecture becomes a medium responding to organic shapes, human forms and functions within it. Where the roof bends to meet the armature, glass planes replace the zinc roof, producing a continuous skylight. The rotation of the second floor allows for better views and privacy. A cantilevering terrace extends from the second floor to the living room. Coming in by the second floor, a slot in the kitchen wall directs the gaze towards the lake. The living-and-dining-room, the bedrooms, a sunroom, and an office are located on the second floor, while the ground floor holds a gymnasium, guest quarters, and a garage. The ground floor has direct access outside via a recessed path with a retaining wall of site rocks.

The architecture of the Gypsy House exemplifies the ideas of interdependent layers (wall-glass-roof-glass-armature), efficiency of use (armature as infra-structural core), and negotiation of means (interior/exterior, source of sunlight).

Photographs: Winka Dubbeldam

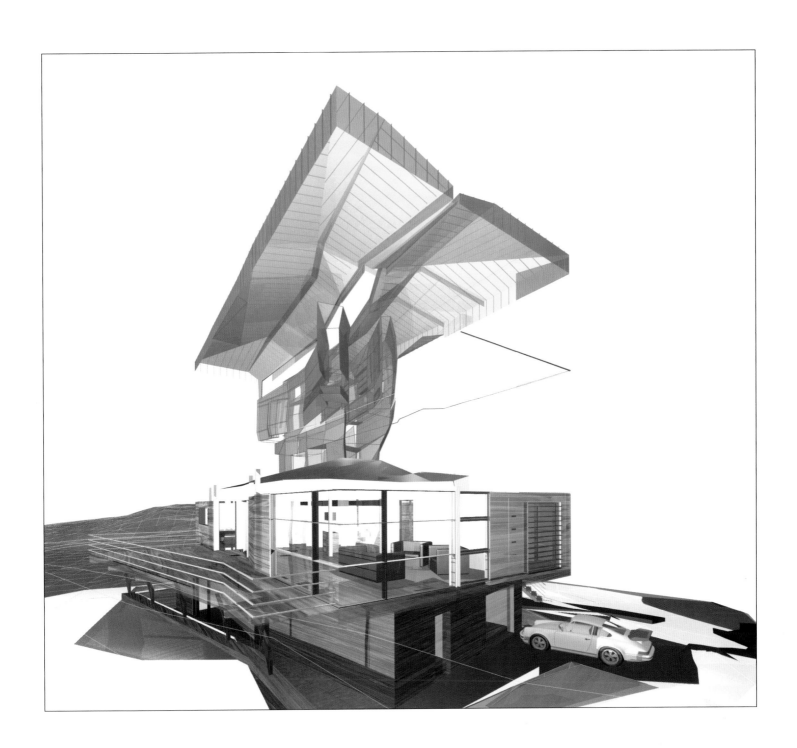

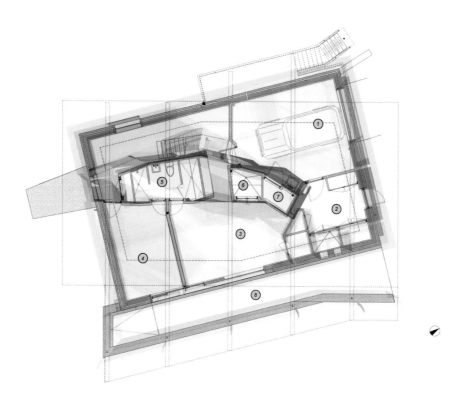

First floor plan

1. Garage
2. Mudroom
3. Gym
4. Guest room
5. Bath / steam room
6. Laundry room
7. Mechanical room
8. Pathway

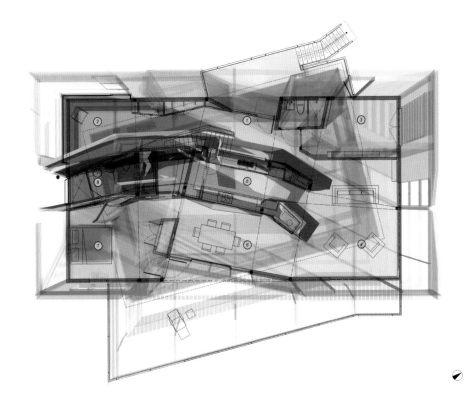

Second floor plan

1. Entrance
2. Sunroom
3. Study
4. Living room
5. Kitchen
6. Dining room
7. Master bedroom
8. Master bathroom

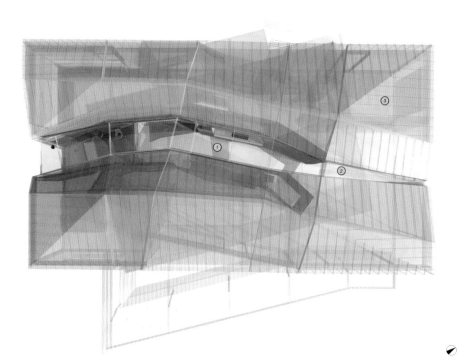

Roof plan

1. Skylight
2. Continuous gutter
3. Zink-clad roof

Performance studies - Armature deflections on "House as pure box"

Armature inserted within "box"

lounging voids

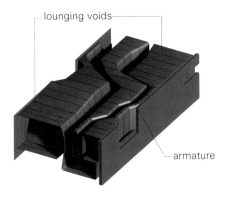

armature

Armature as connective void

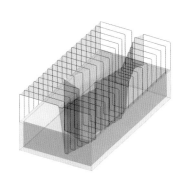

Armature as generative structure:
roof deflection

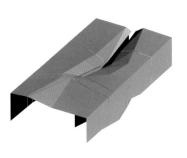

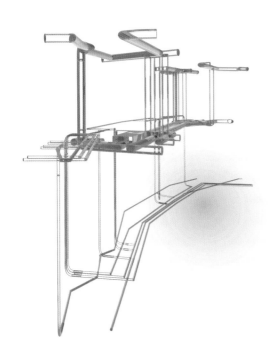

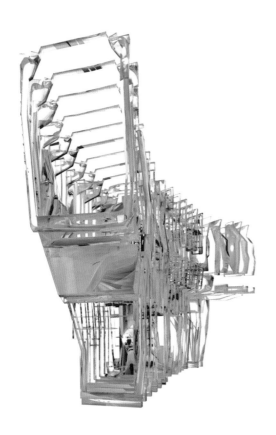

mæ architects
m-House

The m-house project started life in a slightly different form to the mass produced product shown in the majority of the accompanying photographs and drawings. Early in 2003 the client, Tim Pyne approached the architect to design him a weekend home to be set on a plot of land overlooking a wetland estuary in Essex. The sensitivities of the surrounding area meant that permission could only be gained to place two leisure caravans (non-permanent structures) on the site. The client wanted a weekend home that would possess the build, space and design qualities of a contemporary London apartment.

The first task was to research the legal description of a leisure caravan, in order to ascertain the design parameters of the project. The results of this research produced some startling results, firstly that the laws describing this form of accommodation are amazingly simple, because no one had bothered to push the form's possibilities since the late 1940's. Basically a caravan is an accommodation unit that must come to site in no more then two sections, which must be towed into place. These two sections must be fixed together mechanically in order to complete the structure. The dimensional requirements of the structure are defined by the internal or net dimensions. The internal dimensions of 18.2m by 6m gave a generous plan of up to 109.2m^2 with a maximum internal height of 3m; this seemed to offer great possibilities for the project.

The design of the two caravan units, which were to be placed end to end forming one building was governed by the client's wish to have the maximum possible visual and physical connection with the surrounding landscape. One unit was to house living spaces, the other bedroom and bathroom spaces. Each unit would take the form of an off site manufactured, elegant stressed-skin ply structure, (engineered by Techniker). Simple additions of built-in furniture forming kitchen and bathrooms would maintain the open aspect of the interior, which because of the nature of the lining material was taking on the characteristics of a cabin or train carriage.

Excited by the potential of the project the client decided that the scheme should be re-designed as a single unit that could be retailed. He had decided to start a company with the intension of producing units of this type which could take advantage of the off site manufacturing potential and eased planning restrictions which the design delivered.

The architects were asked to produce a rationalized scheme for mass production, which eliminated some of the idiosyncrasies of the one off weekend home project. They produced a robust steel frame solution which had the advantage of being crane deliverable.

The plan is set out with a large kitchen dining area, bathroom, WC, washing room and two cabin-like bedrooms. The interior maintained its timber-lined character, with homely inclusions such as the timber-burning stove, which are augmented with under floor heating through out. The external weathering is achieved in the prototype with profiled aluminum rain cladding and other material treatments such as timber or terracotta depending on site requirements.

Photographs: Morley von Sternberg

Plan

1. External timber ramp
2. Entrance
3. Living area
4. Boiler and washroom
5. Bed 1
6. Bed 2
7. Bathroom
8. W.C
9. External timber deck

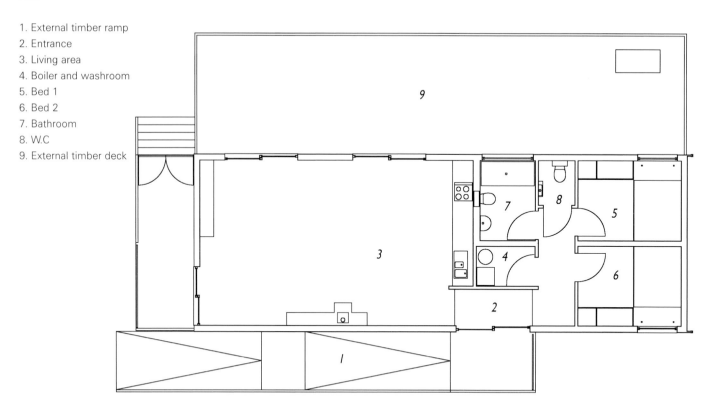

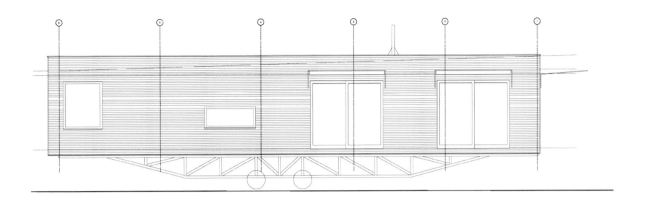

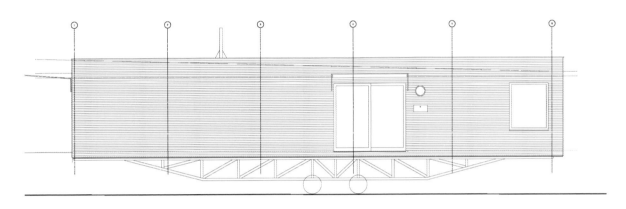

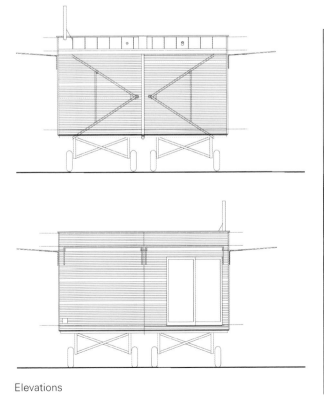

Elevations

The beauty of this building type is that it deals with so many pertinent issues such as affordability, factory production, and the imperative for environmental sustainability. It can sit lightly on green-field sites without causing permanent damage; and allows for the separation of building costs from land costs and so cuts out one of the key cost restrictions to housing.

Kanner architects
Canyon View Office/Guesthouse

Brentwood, California, U.S.A.

Located on a lush hillside behind a main residence, this small structure housing a psychologist's office/guesthouse is just a few steps away from home yet it feels like a protected sanctuary. Solving the problem of an ever-frustrating commute, this home-office offers both privacy and convenience while enhancing the property's value. It also can double as a guesthouse for visiting friends or family. The owners insisted on a minimalist design that was to be flexible, modern, private, warm and contextual.

The structure's highly articulated form is composed of a series of angled cedar wall planes. The "breaking of the box" into a series of angled walls allows the building to more effectively blend into its environment. Each plan angle responds to room function, view corridors, light quality and programmatic flexibility.

The waiting room can also double as a guest room and has its own entrance. The main office space has its own entrance and it can double as a living room. Both spaces have abundant views to the eucalyptus trees and lush landscape. A bathroom, entrance closet and small "kitchenette" round out the program.

Interiors are simple and take a back seat to the views framed by the large wood trimmed windows. Staying with the natural palette of materials expressed on the exterior, the interior's floors are maple and ceilings, doors, windows and cabinetry are vertical grain Douglas fir. Walls are simple white painted drywall and lighting is suspended below the wood purlins on stainless steel cable tacks.

The new landscaping, steps and site walls tie in with the materials used elsewhere on the site. Broken concrete steps and retaining walls, bamboo hedges, red flax, liriope shrubs and young eucalyptus trees will one day mature to create a seamless blend with their older counterparts.

Photographs: John Linden

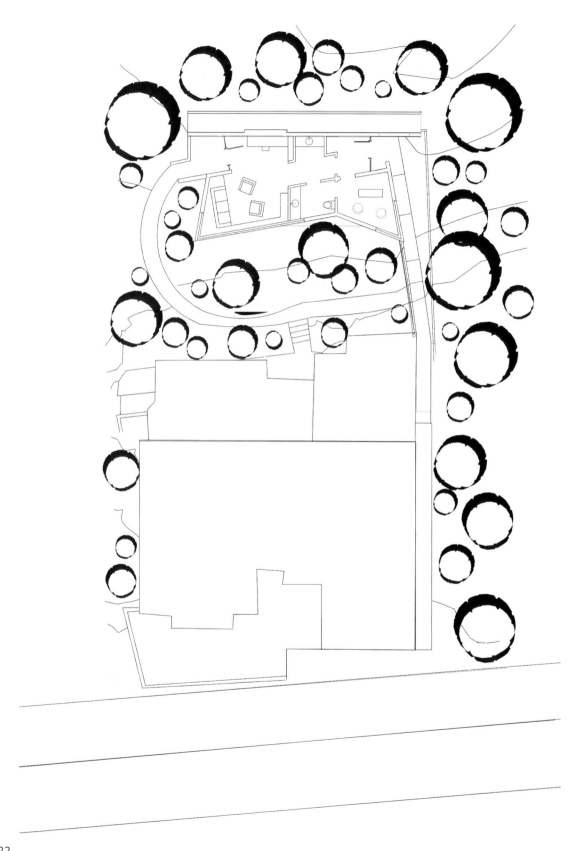

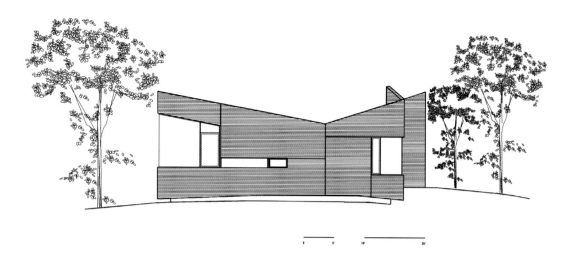

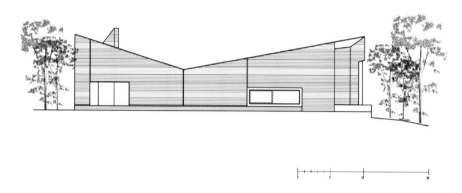

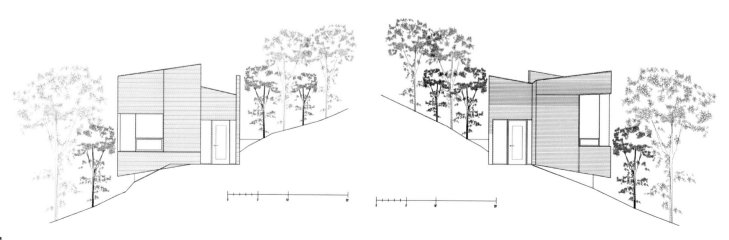

Cross section

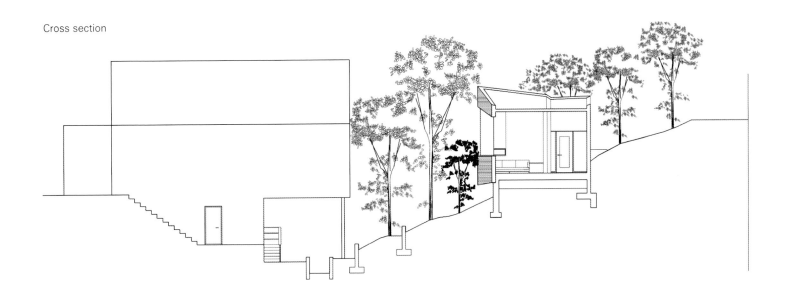

The house's form is composed of a series of angled walls. This fragmented form allows the building to blend into its environment. The specific angles correspond to room functions, views and light qualities.

The ineriors are simple and follow the natural palette of materials of the exterior. Floors are made of maple and ceilings, doors, windows and cabinetry are vertical grain Douglas fir. Walls are simple white painted drywall and lighting is suspended below the wood purlins on stainless steel cable tacks.

gerner °gerner plus, andreas gerner, gerda maria gerner
sued.see

Jois, Burgenland, Austria

The site is located in a very flat, dry and windy area in the east of Austria near lake Neusiedl, which is famous for sailing and windsurfing. The family living there were looking for a site not too far away from Vienna, but also on the country-side. They were well-informed about architecture, architects, materials and alterna-tives to common uses.

It was a very interesting work for the architects, because neither the community nor the people living around it have ever seen such a building especially not as a single-family-dwelling. Even now they call it a UFO, space station or sailing-boat. This term is not so far away, because the shading-systems of the house are made of the same material as on sailing-boats. Every day people come to have a look inside, because they cannot imagine how to live inside such a UFO.

The construction is located along a south-west-ern slope and its width is completely open diagonally, southwards to the lake. The northern side is closed, and the remaining exterior skin is formed as a continuous running shell of bonded, sheet metal-covered finished elements. The main storey extends far over the terrain through a cleft in its edge.

In constructive terms, this part is developed as a reinforced-concrete table supported by V-tubes. For the roofed area, a pool wrapped in glass was planned. The construction's form and position are modulated in consideration of the west winds that can reach gale force. The project was completed within less than ten months after the first site meeting.

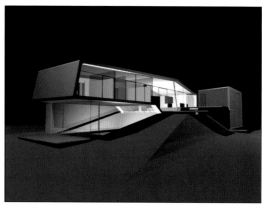
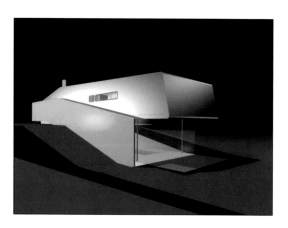

Photographs: Manfred Seidl

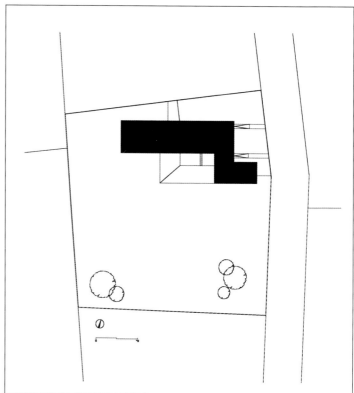

Site plan

The house is located along a south-western slope and its width is completely open diagonally, southwards to the lake and closed at the northern side. The main storey extends far over the terrain through a cleft in its edge.

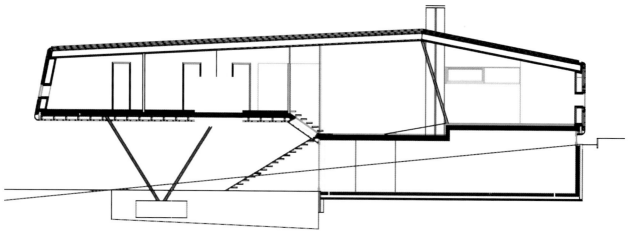

Longitudinal section

1. Bedroom
2. Children´s bedroom
3. Living room
4. Kitchen - dining
5. Bathroom
6. Shower
7. WC
8. Entrance
9. Office
10. Terrace

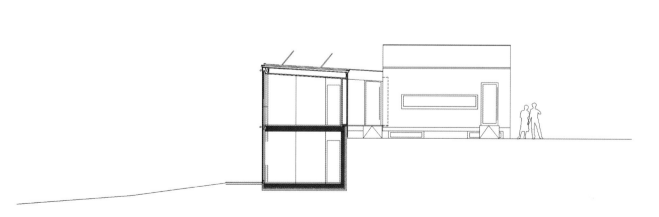

Cross section

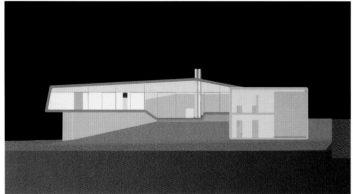

South elevation

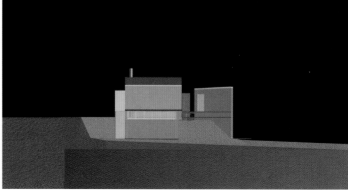

West elevation

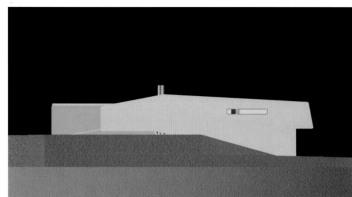

North elevation

East elevation

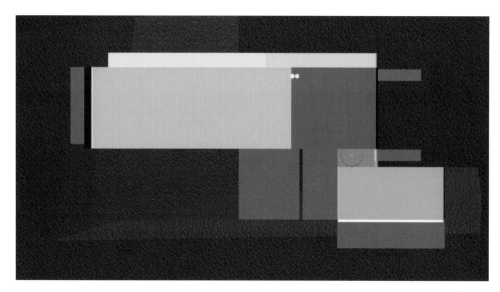

Roof plan

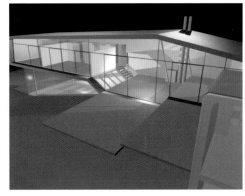

The community and the people living around it had never before seen such a building especially not as a single-family-dwelling. Even now they call it a UFO, space station or sailing-boat. Every day people come to have a look inside, because they cannot imagine how to live inside such a UFO.

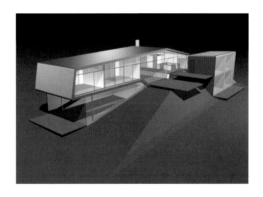

Álvaro Siza
House in Oudenbourg

Oudenbourg, Belgium

The project consists in the saving, renovation, and extension of an existing farm into living spaces and an art gallery. The three basic volumes in a U-shaped form around a patio were taken as the theme for the scheme of the entire project. In this way, a first open space with a semi-public character identifies with the history of the site, while a second patio relates to the new buildings and creates a more private atmosphere. Integration here means "doing what is still existing" or "building with tradition": unpretentious volumes with the same geometric section as the existing ones are connected onto each other.

But where the house and the nearly 200 year old stables were built in masonry with roof tiles, the new extensions distinguish themselves in materials and detail. Identifying with the history of interior and landscape paintings as from the Flemish primitives, well-proportioned openings toward the landscape bring a studied light into the interior. On the contrary, an oblique window in blue hard stone, along with façades in western red cedar and a lead-covered roof, explain that the new extensions aren't related to some formal expression but to the meaning of the integration of time, of disappearance, and of well-loved craftsmanship. The patina of materials, the slightly changing grey colours with the passage of time, and the will of being humble in front of the big flat landscape of these "Polders" combine to express a certain attitude of context and building.

The existing buildings carry other specific interpretations of space and its expression. In the art gallery the reflection of the zenithal light in combination with a solitary column reveal the structuring of the space in which works of contemporary art have to find their place and meaning. The elaboration of the remaining façades and roofs talk about rural craftsmanship and the idea of using this tradition to make new interpretations.

Besides the fact of building in the Flemish landscape and the particular history of the site, the project intends to create some new perspectives for the owners and their familial relationship with this area, for the site asks for new interventions and for an art of building apart from that which is today too much related to formal and photographic consumption.

Photographs: Duccio Malagamba

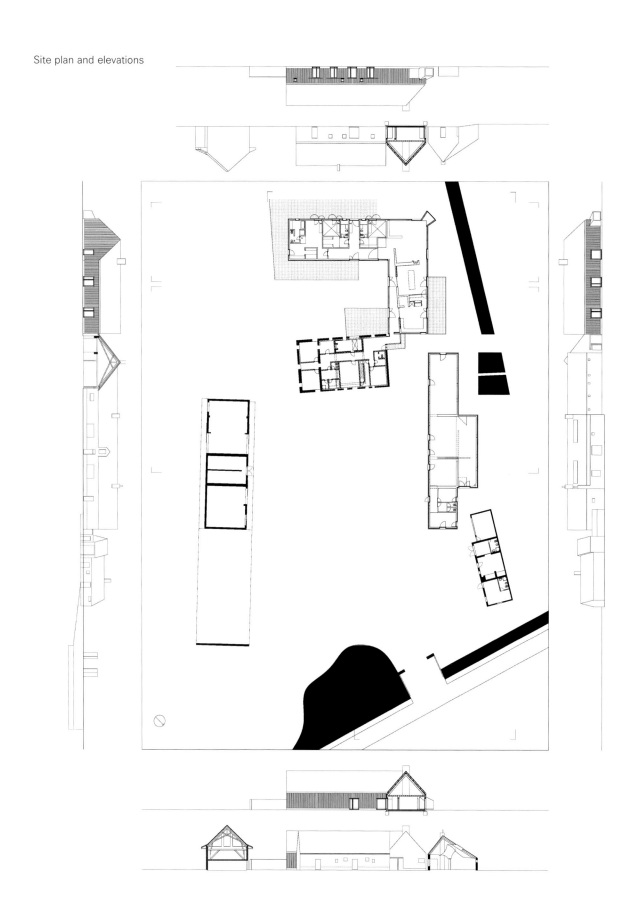

Art Gallery

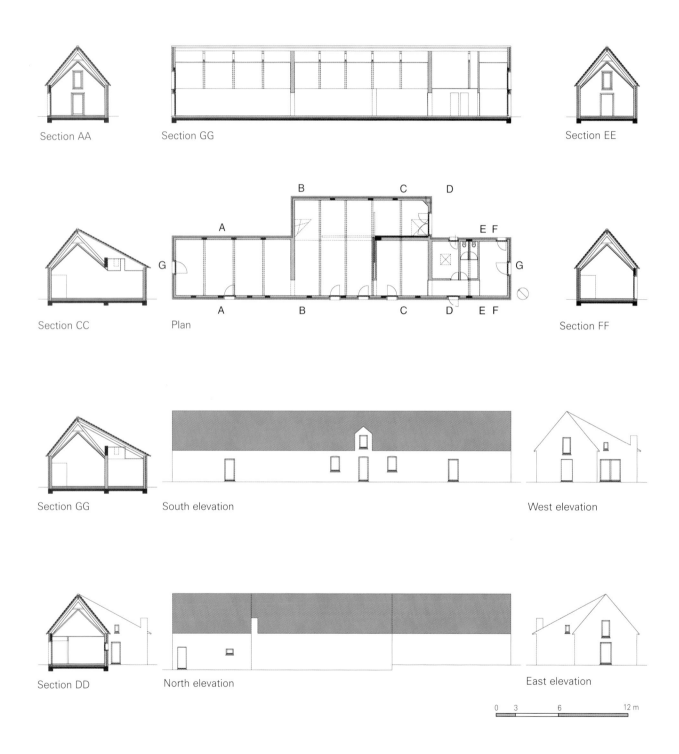

Section AA

Section GG

Section EE

Section CC

Plan

Section FF

B   C   D

A

E F

G   A   B   C   D   E F   G

Section GG

South elevation

West elevation

Section DD

North elevation

East elevation

0   3   6   12 m

House

South elevation

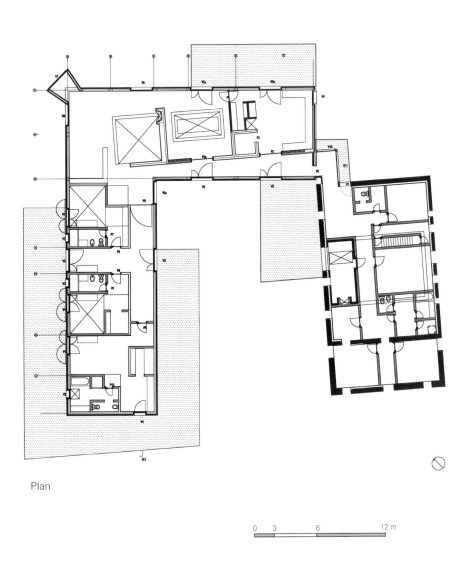

Plan

0   3   6   12 m

Bernard Quirot & Olivier Vichard
Convercey House

Grachaux (Haute-Saône), France

Built for a landscape architect and his wife, this house is a sort of "machine to capture the landscape".

It is narrow, entirely stretched between its two extremities and the parts of the landscape it frames. It is elevated on pilotis to acquire the beautiful, long views over the plain.

Throughout the simple, open plan one can see the entire length of the house, but this longitudinal dynamic is interrupted twice to define the main living spaces.

In the dining corner, two large opposing bay windows create a transversal axis allowing the landscape to cross the house from east to west. In the living room, the tallest ceiling along with the chimney creates a vertical axis emphasized by a roof light above.

The steel structure, mounted in a fortnight, gives the general silhouette a simplicity and lightness, minimizing the project's impact on the site. The house appears to meet the natural terrain at only one point - the entrance - and, like a Roman weighing-scales, the work finds its equilibrium from this point: a large narrow volume detached from the earth of the living room side, a shorter but wider volume on the bedroom side.

Inside, the partition depth is sufficient for storing heaters and book-shelving in the niches, in order to maximize the spatial fluidity of the house.

This project is the result of a perfect client-architect agreement of intentions, but its construction was without doubt only made possible by the total and exceptional absence of building regulations in this tiny portion of French territory.

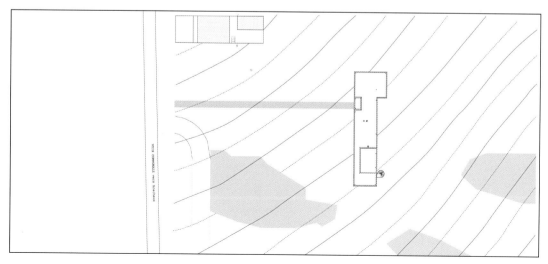

Photographs: Luc Boegly

Axonometric

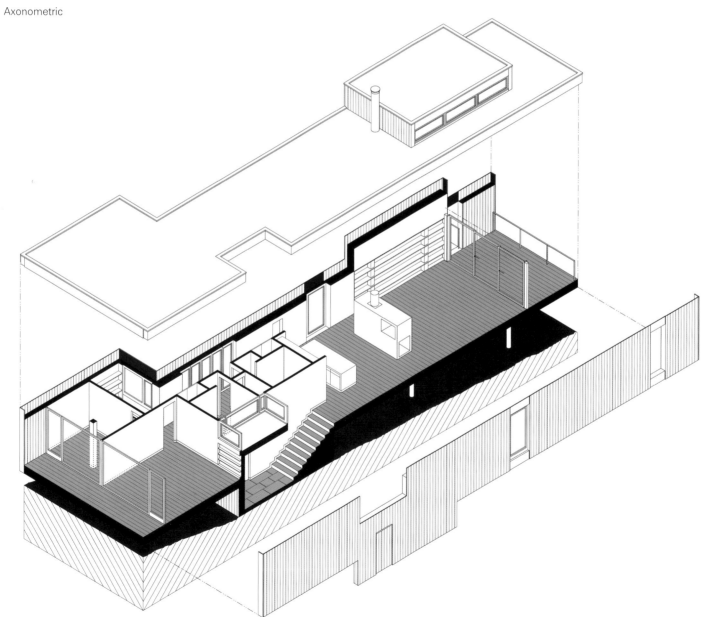

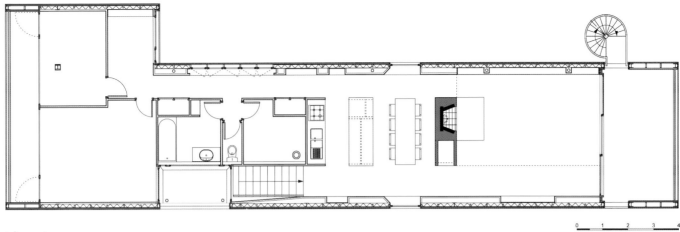

First floor plan

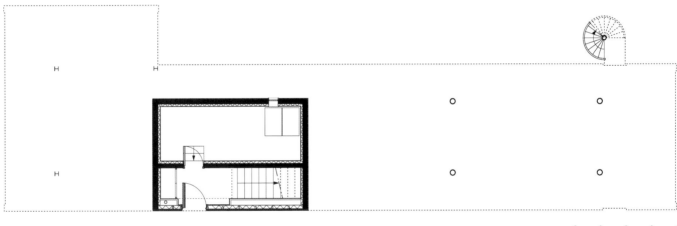

Ground floor plan - entrance

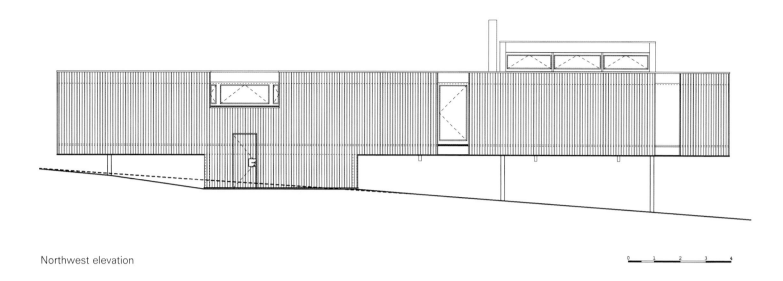

Northwest elevation

0   1   2   3   4

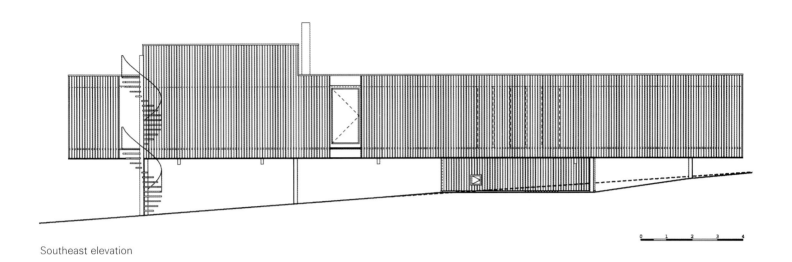

Southeast elevation

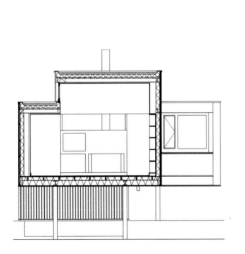

Cross section

Throughout the simple, open plan one can see the entire length of the house, but this longitudinal dynamic is interrupted twice to define the main living spaces.

HERTL.ARCHITEKTEN
Seidl House

Molln, Austria

From the start, the prospect of building a private house in the Limestone Alps, one of the most extensive woodland districts of Upper Austria, suggested a timber construction as an obvious solution. Wooden clapboard cladding on the façades and the roof, plus a short span of time, will have the buildings wrapped in a coat of subtle grays, which will allow them to establish a simple and natural presence in the landscape.

Reinterpreting the distribution of the region's vernacular rural structures around an open yard, the two very slim parallel volumes face each other from opposite sides of a sheltered open space which they define; at the same time, this leaves open and accentuates the two most remarkable view directions: The distant valley towards the south and the majestic mountains rising close by to the north. This theme has been echoed throughout the distribution and design details of the living areas.

The main ground floor space is intended to be read as an uninterrupted pipe lying open at both ends. Nevertheless the elongated solidium is divided longitudinally into a narrow functional and work area (washroom, laundry, kitchen and storage), and a wider living room area.

The seemingly simple special organization corresponds to the original functional arrangement of traditional rural buildings, which has also determined the passive house concept, with a heat pump and controlled ventilation.

The slope in the land has made it possible to provide the cellar with plentiful natural light that enters through the huge glazed opening at the open northern end. The north façade is in fact almost entirely glass, rising the full height of the building; the cellar digs back into the land and is almost as long as the whole building.

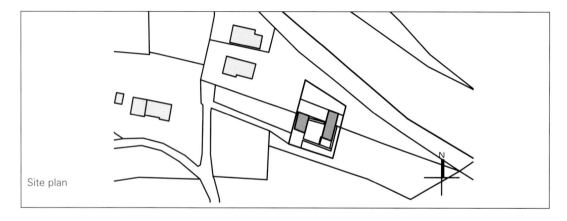

Site plan

Photographs: Paul Ott

Basement

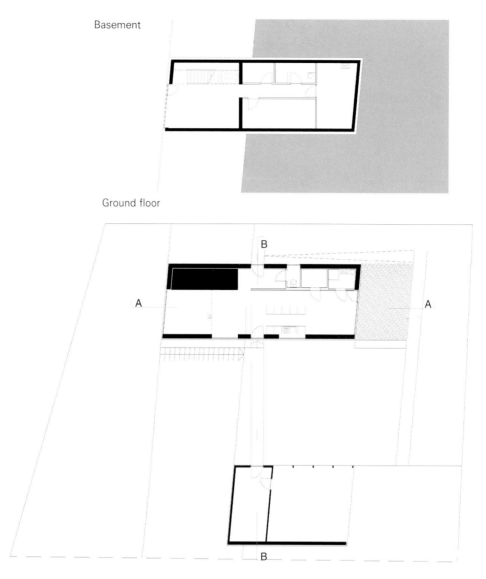

Ground floor

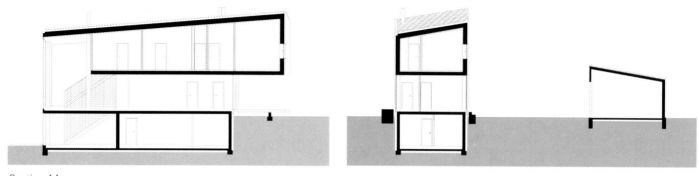

Section AA

Section BB

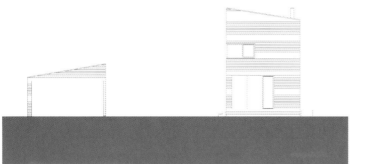

South elevation

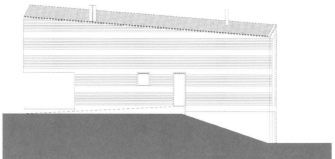

East elevation

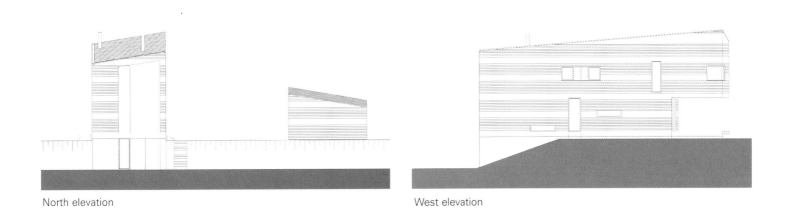

North elevation

West elevation

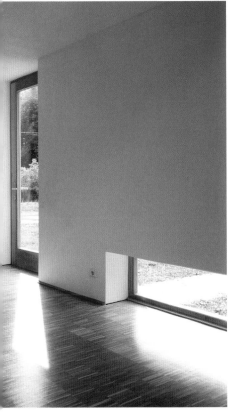

175

XTEN Architecture
Vhouse

Dixie Canyon, Los Angeles, California, USA

The Vhouse is located on a hillside street, set amongst tightly spaced small-scale stucco houses without any remarkable architectural qualities. The sloping canyon hillside to the rear of the site however, with its walnut and conifer trees, offered a wonderful environment for an open architecture linking inside and outside space.

Instead of a multistory volume that would dominate the setting, the architects chose a low courtyard installation that fits into the canyon plot like a pavilion. Four thick bearing walls are oriented perpendicular to the hillside and follow the site lines of the V-shaped lot. A series of laminated wood beams clear span between these walls and allow for large areas of the facade to open to the landscape. The folds and cantilevers of the roof geometry are articulated to respond to the specific conditions of the site.

The courtyard is planned as an outdoor room around which the different types of day and nighttime living are organized. Several sets of glass doors create a soft threshold between the living area and the courtyard. Direct access from the open kitchen allows for outdoor dining and entertaining throughout the year, while secondary openings in the bearing walls allow for access from the bedrooms in the mornings.

Inside, the four bearing walls define three distinct program zones. The central zone is planned as a single cohesive open space that offers, for the most part, a transparent indoor/outdoor living space. Flanking this area are two wings that house the bedrooms and more private spaces of the program.

The detailing and materiality of the house is minimal yet indivisibly bound to its architectural concept. The thick bearing walls are clad in wide redwood planks that wrap continuously from exterior to interior and extend the landscape deep into the interior of the house through vertical glass panels. In contrast to these volumetric walls, the soft façades are treated as a surface texture of finely ribbed redwood slats spaced between floor to roof glass with fir framing. This framing is in turn connected to the spacing of the exposed roof structure, generating a series of continuous lines that articulate the interior space while also framing the exterior courtyard and canyon hillside beyond.

Photographs: Art Gray

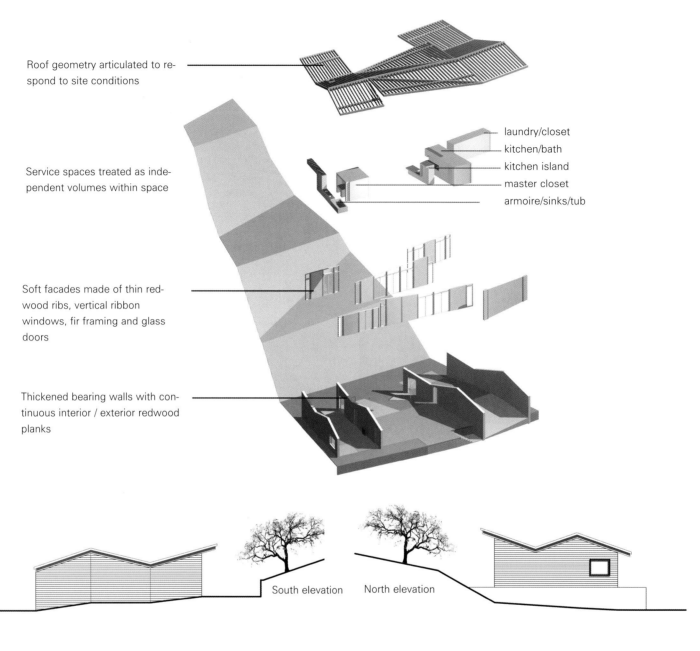

Roof geometry articulated to respond to site conditions

Service spaces treated as independent volumes within space

laundry/closet
kitchen/bath
kitchen island
master closet
armoire/sinks/tub

Soft facades made of thin redwood ribs, vertical ribbon windows, fir framing and glass doors

Thickened bearing walls with continuous interior / exterior redwood planks

South elevation   North elevation

East-west section

EAST-WEST SECTION

Roof slopes down to street for privacy and angles back up for hillside views

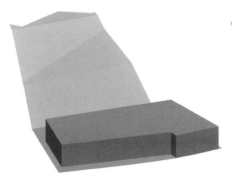

Maximum site coverage, given city set-backs

Concentration to street = larger garden area

Two wings with courtyard = flow to lands-cape

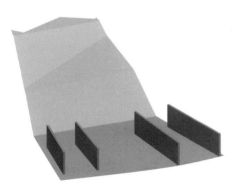

Four fin walls = three distinct program zones

Canyon landscape = roof-scape

Wood canopy supported by blades

Site strategy

Corners are folded up to open main living space to light and landscape beyond

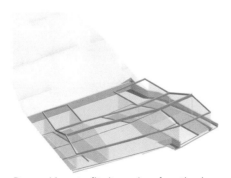

Beams hinge to fit site and roof section is subtracted to create open courtyard

Full roofscape with all primary beams and secondary framing

Ground floor plan

1. Master bedroom
2. Bath
3. Closet
4. Study
5. Patio
6. Living - dining
7. Kitchen
8. Bath
9. Entry
10. Pantry
11. Patio
12. Bedroom
13. Closet
14. Carport

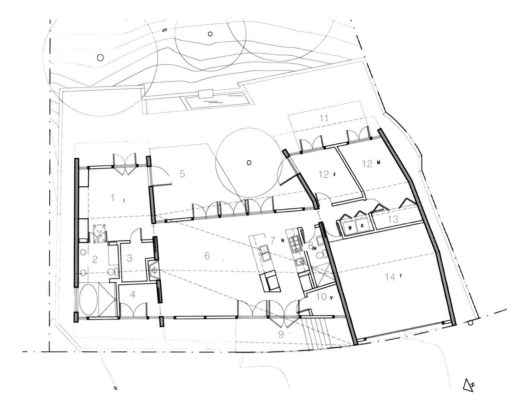

West elevation

East elevation

The folds and cantilevers of the roof geometry are articulated to respond to specific site conditions: turned down at the street edge to create privacy; folded up above the bearing walls to gain light from the sides; and sloping up again at the rear of the site to open the interior spaces to the hillside through full-height glass panels.

Service elements such as closets and cabinets are treated as independent elements fixed to the bearing walls but cut at a height of eight-feet so that the exposed roof framing is continuous, floating above them.

RCR Aranda Pigem Vilalta arquitectes

M-Lidia House

Montagut, Girona, Spain

This house was built on a simple, straightforward site with good views. It was designed with a limited budget for a young couple without children.

The building consists of a metallic box structure with thin walls and glass protected by metallic mesh that opens the space towards the exterior, creating gaps that are perfect for managing the wind.

A concrete slab was used for the foundation, and a steel frame for the metallic structure. The metallic box was assembled in the workshop, and rests on walls that form an enclosed, partly underground area that contains the garage.

In section, with all the services grouped together, the interior space is defined by the thin or the thick walls. The space can be divided in three or left open, depending on the placement of the glass walls in the gaps. These change the perception of space in relation to its size, relative emptiness or fullness and its exterior-interior qualities.

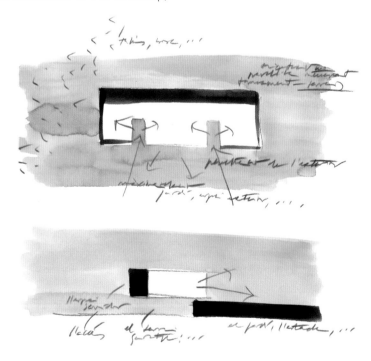

Photographs: Eugeni Pons

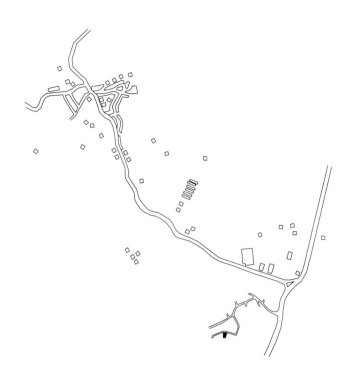

Site plan

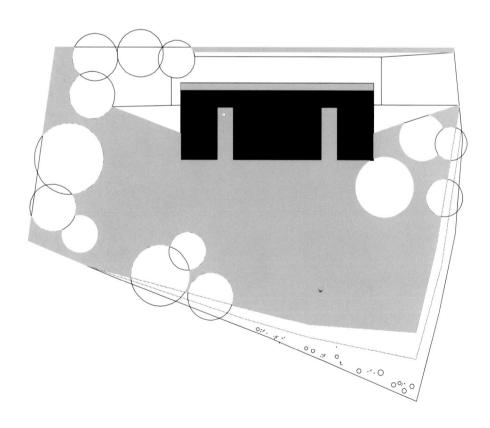

First floor

B C

A   A

B C

Front elevation

Section AA

Section BB

Section CC

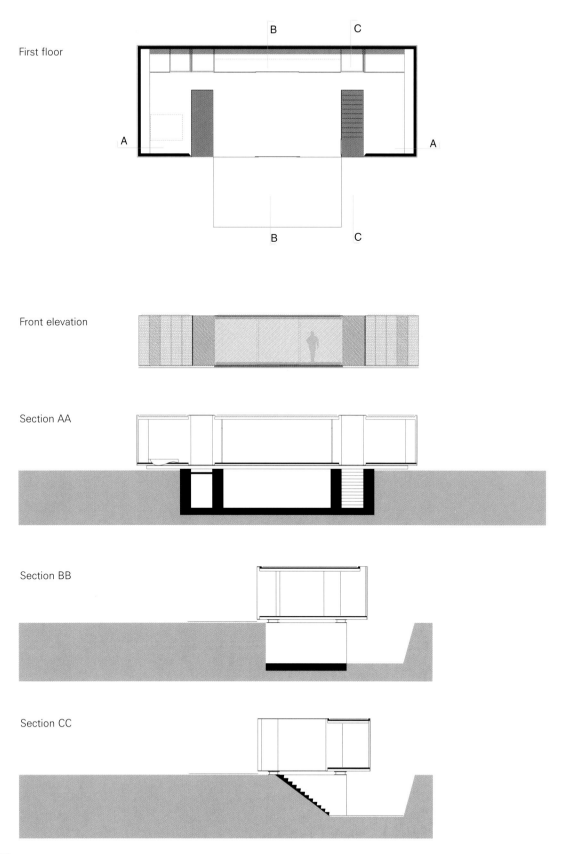

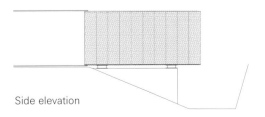

Side elevation

June 21   September 21   December 21   March 21

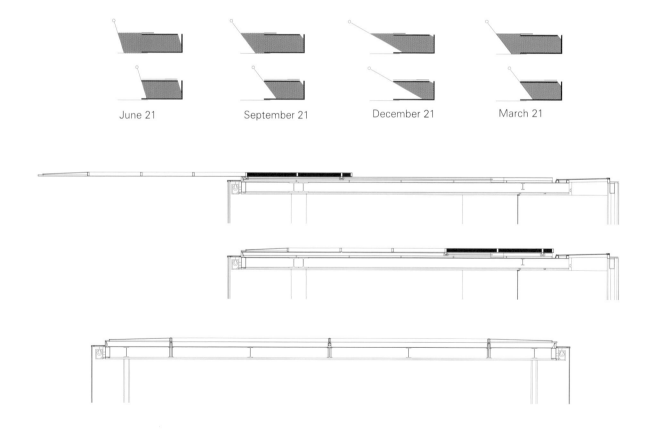

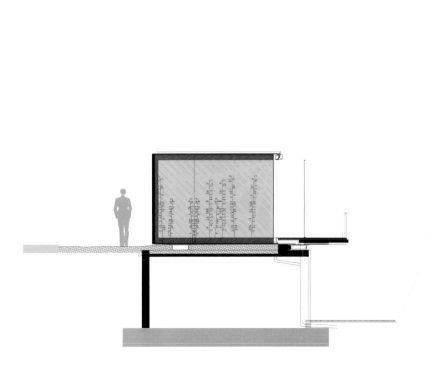

Arkkitehtisuunnittelu Huttunen & Lipasti

Villa Linnanmäki

Somerniemi, Finland

The villa is located on a narrow strip of woodland that separates the open agricultural terrain from a lake; it consists in a dwelling unit of modest size and a separate sauna cabin. These constructions are sited on opposite sides of a pathway that winds its way through a group of birch trees that brighten the more solemn context of pine forests. The path comes down from the edge of the field, passes between the house and the sauna cabin and continues to the lakeshore. The house offers a generous open façade towards the lake, as opposed to the other three sides, that are almost blank, facing the woodland and the fields.

All the walls are sided with the plentiful local pine wood. The traditional protective black oil finish of the timber buildings replicates the dark tones of the edge of the forest. The open lakeside façade reveals the warm golden tones of the same timber showing its natural color, which predominates in the interiors as well as the terrace-deck that extends a few yards in front of the house. This functions as a welcome addition to the living room, which is relatively compact.

Immediately in front of the house, the birch trees shelter the building's open front from the excessive sun, and the foliage repeats the honey tones of the interior walls; otherwise the plot has been left in its natural state, an untouched context that the buildings are inscribed upon with candid frankness. The interior space is divided by a masonry wall, around which the water system has been centered, together with the heating appliance, a wood-burning storage heater.

The façades of the upper floor module have been sided with the same metal sheeting as the roof, integrating the volume into the lower floor and maintaining the proximity to the ground that characterizes the buildings when they are approached from the rear. Seen from the front, the upper floor has a totally different geometry, only the golden interior, which glows from the balcony towards the lake, reveals the identity of the two bodies. This space contains the master bedroom, which overlooks the surrounding landscape from a slight vantage point.

Photographs: Marko Huttunen

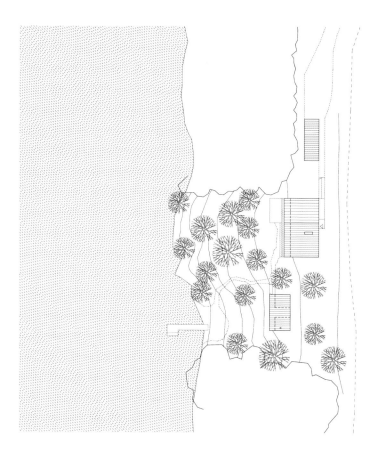

Site plan

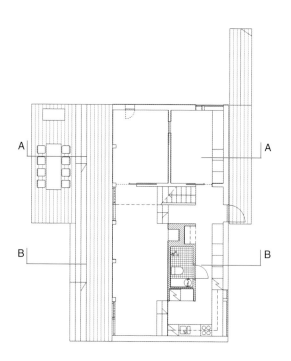

House - Ground floor

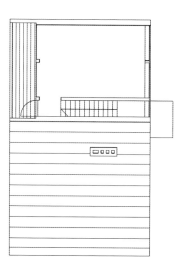

House - First floor

House - West elevation

House - North elevation

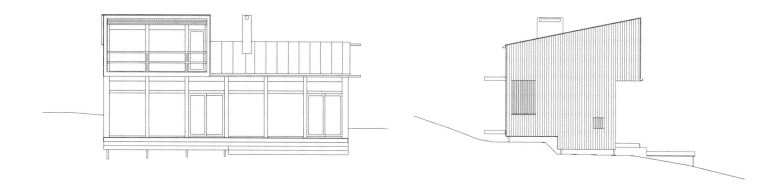

House - East elevation

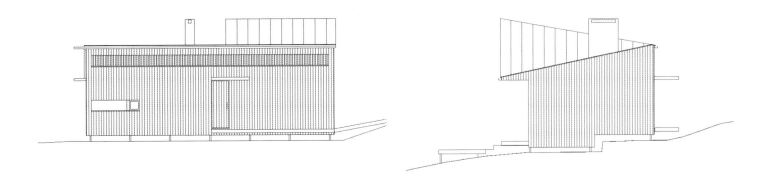

House - South elevation

House - Section AA

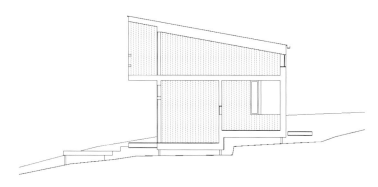

House - Section BB

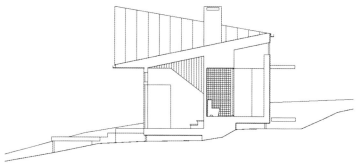

Sauna - Plan

Sauna - Section

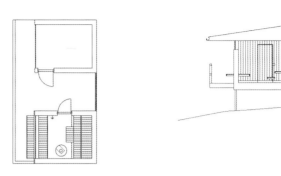

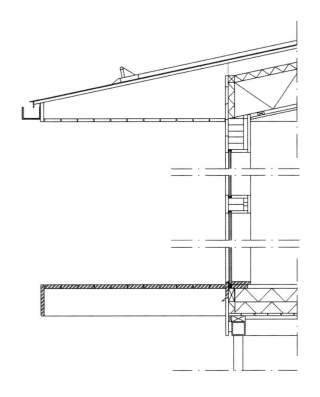

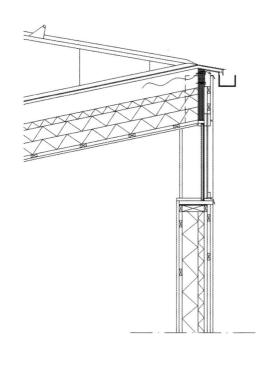

Lorcan O'Herlihy Architects

Jai House

Calabasas, California, USA

The Jai House sits on a gently sloping 4 acre site overlooking the Santa Monica Mountains. It is a study of the interaction between building and landscape and celebrates an architecture of removal by stripping away visual and spatial excess, revealing an authenticity of construction and craft.

The building is designed to blur the boundary between landscape and structure. The primary level which houses the main public spaces is conceived of as a linear bar which acts as a buffer to Mulholland Highway. This level engages the earth at one end and floats above the landscape at the other. The primary level, which opens completely to the views and canyon beyond, houses the living, dining, kitchen, two bedrooms, yoga studio and outdoor rooms. Extending the interaction between inside/out-

side is a 75-foot lap pool that slices through the building and the public spaces. The pool and deck are an extension of the living room.

The upper volume, which is at a 90 degree angle to the primary level, houses the master bedroom suite that frames the view towards the Santa Monica Mountains. The bathroom area is open to the master bedroom. The client's programmatic brief stipulated that the house include space for exclusive yoga retreats. The yoga room is at the east end of the house and separated by an outdoor room. The architectural solution seamlessly engages the interior designed in collaboration with Julie Piatt. The exterior material of the primary level is smooth troweled plaster with glass walls. The upper level is wrapped in skin of metal mesh.

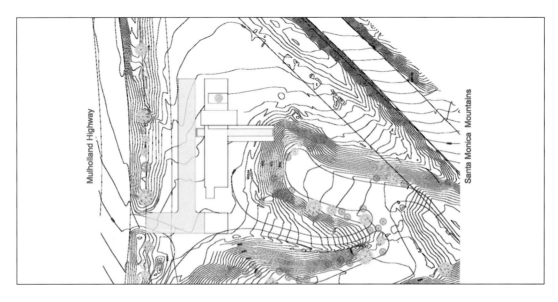

Photographs: Michael Weschler

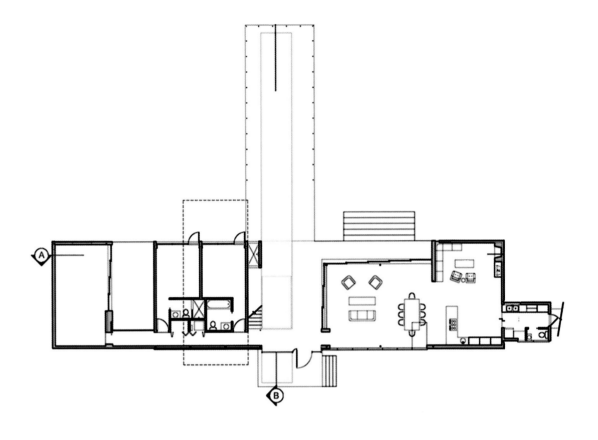

Ground floor

1. Living room
2. Dining room
3. Kitchen
4. Family room
5. Laundry
6. Powder room
7. Pool
8. Entrance
9. Bedroom 1
10. Bedroom 2
11. Patio
12. Yoga room

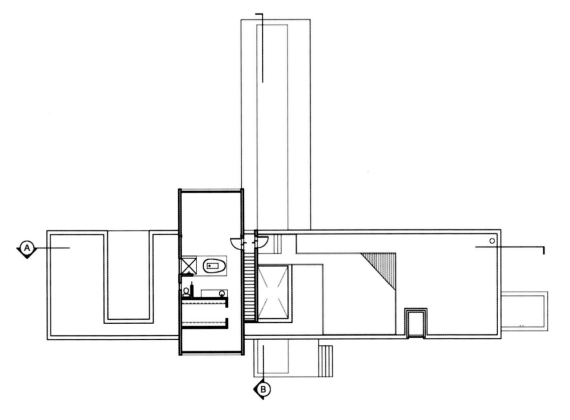

First floor

1. Master bedroom
2. Bathroom
3. Closet
4. Office
5. Deck

The lap pool slices through the public spaces of the building and functions as an extension of the living room, reinforcing the interaction between interior and exterior.

Section B

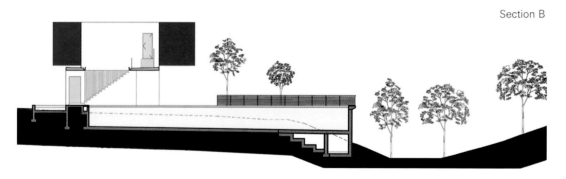

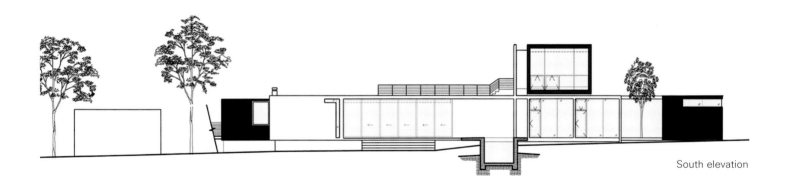

South elevation

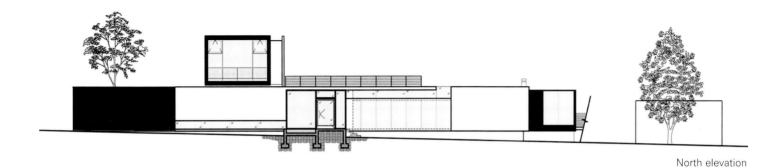

North elevation

217

hobby a., Wolfgang Maul & Walter Schuster
House for Eva and Fritz

Bergheim/Salzburg , Austria

Being a young self-employed photographer and an advertising agent the owners asked for a home that reflects the flexible, mobile and temporary character of their profession and that, nevertheless, fits into the surroundings and is more charming than an ordinary, soulless trailer. The architects' primary objective was a monolithic block with a homogeneous exterior design that corresponds with the industrial context in the neighbourhood. As first experiments with a coating of polyurethane or fibreglass respectively failed, a prestressed membrane structure from PVC coated polyester highdensity yarn was found the ideal material. Just imagine a house in Emma Peel's appealing gear.

This smooth skin covers a light construction of twelve pieces of insulated woodwork that were prefabricated at the carpenter's and assembled at the site. The wooden elements consist of orientated span boards (OSB) both inside and outside which are mounted onto the supporting wooden stays with insulation in-between. Allowing three centimetres of airing, the synthetic membrane is stretched smoothly over the rounded edges of the building. Only then the window-outlets are cut with Stanley-knives and the edges of the membrane pulled in again. This processing does not need any kind of metal sheets, which results in a homogeneous body. The semi-permeable membrane shows the same characteristics as the well-known material Gore-Tex, humidity is transported to the outside but not the other way round.

A different story is the rounded edges and corners of the house: ever so simple as effective. A quarter-segment of a polocal tube with a diameter of 50 centimetres each forms an elevation. The corners take up 14 elements of exact sphere segments altogether, which were moulded for that very purpose.

The aesthetics of these unusual materials flash light onto an architectural taboo. Synthetic materials surround us, whether in shops, cars or our workplaces. Only architecture pretends that there have not been any new materials since Vitruvius. Embarrassed, we conceal the entire choice of contemporary materials, such as Styrofoam insulation, PU-foam or silicon-synthetic resin, behind plastering, natural-stone facades and wooden grating.

Emanating from some Austrian regions, an ideology has won recognition that propagates the restoration of genuine wood-constructions, which actually consist of epoxy-soaked wood-shavings. This house is a thorn in the side of the theory of regionalism as a confinement to form and/or material. Should regionalism be of any relevance in a global context, it is to be reconsidered thoroughly and without the least fear. Otherwise it might fall back on a new provincialism sooner or later.

Photographs: Fritz Hauswirth, hobby.a

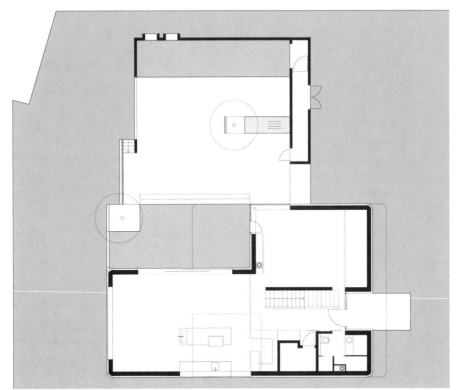

Ground floor

The architects' primary objective was a monolithic block with a homogeneous exterior design that corresponds with the industrial context in the neighbourhood. A prestressed membrane structure from PVC coated polyester highdensity yarn was found the ideal material.

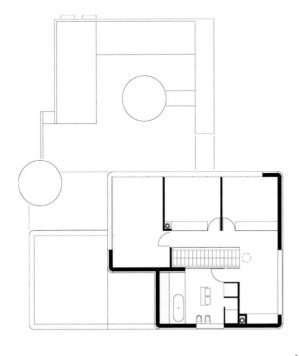

0 1   5 m

First floor

South elevation

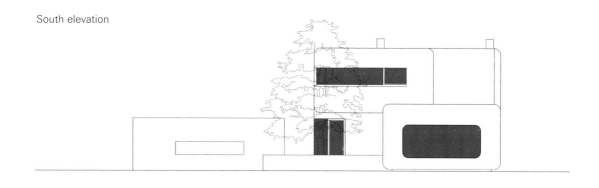

Section

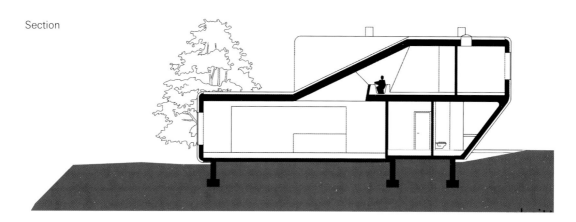

225

Satoshi Okada architects
House in Mt. Fuji

Narusawa Village, Mt. Fuji, Japan

The house is a weekend villa for inviting guests. The site is situated among the broadleaf trees in the northern foothills of Mt. Fuji, 1200m above sea level. It extends from southwest to northeast, inclining gently with a mean gradient of approximately 1/10, facing two roads on its northeastern and southeastern boundaries respectively. Its ground, molded out of lava flows back in antiquity, undulates to a great extent in the east-west direction. Peace and calm reign over the area, only to be broken by an adjacent log-house on the west.

The client requested to build a small house in order to appreciate its surrounding nature. The building was brought closer to the northwestern boundary, offering a pleasant sight filled with sunlight, trees, along with a panoramic rise and fall of the land stretching out to the southeast, and also shielding as much as possible the daily sight of the neighboring log-house on the west. The house volume is divided into two realms by a diagonally folded wall. One is a big space for living and accommodating guests; the other contains the bedrooms and a bathroom. In the living area, the ceiling height gradually comes down from 5.3m to 3.8m in accordance with the sloping roof. Beneath the loft, dining and kitchen are placed as a compressed space with a 2.0m ceiling height.

On the exterior, along the folded wall, the sloping roof is designed to follow the silhouette of the terrain as it is seen from the southeast roads in order to control the building scale in the landscape.

The structure consists of a wood-frame construction. The folded wall is effective against wind loads to the huge wall of the living room. The bathroom, a small box extruded from the main body of the building because of its high humidity, structurally anchors the hall, the tall void beside. The outer wall is made of Japanese cedar stained in black, the color of lava, for the memory of the site.

Photographs: Hiroyuki Hirai

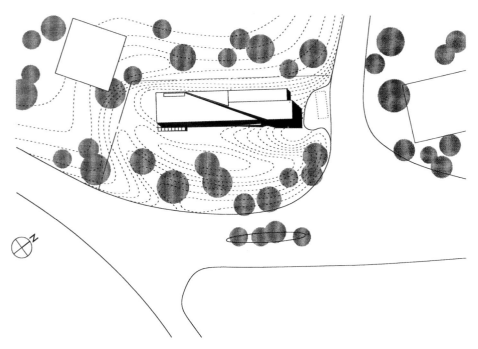

Site plan

On the premises are a number of deciduous trees such as Japanese beech or magnolia. A forest of white birch extends towards north. In the landscape, between the leaves above and the turf floor, the villa stands like a ground upheaval of the site, where the black lava has slept since the ancient times. It also provides a dark band between the greens, where the blackness represents "a shadow in the forest."

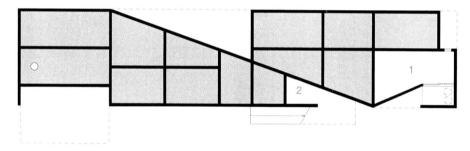

Basement

1. Storage
2. Machine

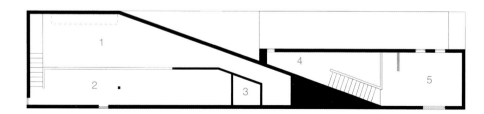

Ground Floor

1. Living
2. Terrace
3. Kitchen
4. Ramp
5. Entrance
6. Hall
7. Bathroom
8. Balcony
9. Tatami-room
10. Service yard

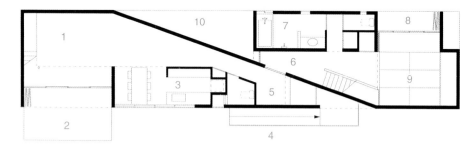

First Floor

1. Void
2. Loft
3. Void
4. Void
5. Bedroom

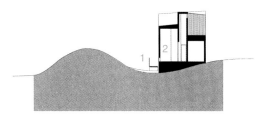

Cross Section

1. Ramp
2. Entrance

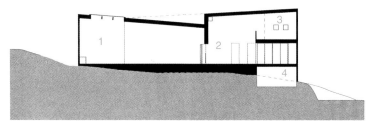

Longitudinal Section

1. Living
2. Hall
3. Bedroom
4. Storage

From a relatively dark entrance, one goes through a tall and narrow, but dim space towards the taller, broader and lighter space along the folded wall, which is lit from a narrow skylight. The hall of the bedrooms represents the space of the latter half of a day. The narrow end portion has a small window beneath the ceiling, from which the afternoon sunlight shines on the opposite white wall to turn its color into orange.